The Unmaking of the Chinese Working Class

HUNDRED FLOWERS

In 1956, seven years after his victory in China's Communist Revolution, Mao Zedong extended an invitation to the country's intelligentsia: "Let a hundred flowers bloom, let a hundred different schools of thought contend." As criticism of the Chinese Communist Party swelled, the Hundred Flowers project morphed into something cynical, known as the Anti-Rightist Campaign. As a result, many who had, in good faith, produced texts and essays critical of the party faced repression; many careers were destroyed.

Verso's Hundred Flowers series aims to fulfill Mao's promise in earnest by publishing writing on China from the mainland, the diaspora, and elsewhere. Once a key American ally, China has emerged over the course of this century as the only serious challenger to US global economic hegemony. Yet China remains largely opaque to the West, which is too often ignorant of both the country's history and its contemporary internal dynamics. Books, newspaper articles, and magazine essays abound but at best present simplistic views of China; at worst, these accounts are misleading or scaremongering. Hundred Flowers offers a more nuanced perspective to facilitate serious debate in analyzing China's past, present, and future.

Other titles in this series available from Verso Books:

Involution by the Gonglao Collective
The Women by Yan Lianke

The Unmaking of the Chinese Working Class

How Communism Built a Capitalist Superpower

Teemu Ruskola

VERSO
London • New York

First published by Verso 2026

The manufacturer's authorized representative in the EU for product safety (GPSR) is LOGOS EUROPE, 9 rue Nicolas Poussin, 17000, La Rochelle, France
Contact@logoseurope.eu

1 3 5 7 9 10 8 6 4 2

Verso
UK: 6 Meard Street, London W1F 0EG
US: 207 East 32nd Street, New York, NY 10016
versobooks.com

Verso is the imprint of New Left Books

ISBN-13: 978-1-83674-136-7
ISBN-13: 978-1-83674-138-1 (US EBK)
ISBN-13: 978-1-83674-137-4 (UK EBK)

British Library Cataloguing in Publication Data
A catalogue record for this book is available from the British Library

Library of Congress Cataloging-in-Publication Data
A catalog record for this book is available from the Library of Congress

Typeset in Fournier by Hewer Text UK Ltd, Edinburgh
Printed and bound by CPI Group (UK) Ltd, Croydon CR0 4YY

To David L. Eng

Contradiction is universal and absolute; it is present in the process of development of all things and permeates every process from beginning to end.

—Mao Zedong, "On Contradiction"

Someone once said that it is easier to imagine the end of the world than the end of capitalism.

—Fredric Jameson, "Future City"

Contents

Preface

In many ways, this book grows out of my personal and intellectual biography. Most broadly stated, it is a study of changing forms of capitalism and socialism, and of the critical role China has played in their global transformations. I am a comparativist by training as well as life experience, having divided my life and academic career among three continents: Europe, North America, and Asia. I grew up in Northern Finland within a stone's throw from the Iron Curtain and the Arctic Circle, a place frozen in time and space as much by the winds of the Cold War as by subzero currents blowing from the north. Globalization as we know it was beyond anyone's imagination, but I was as determined to escape my parochial existence as Madame Bovary was to get out of Normandy. I eventually landed a scholarship at Stanford University (which was also where I first encountered Emma Bovary, in a literature seminar, the year after I fled Finland). At Stanford I studied Chinese history and philosophy, and then law at Yale. California, my first academic home, could hardly have been farther away from where I grew up, yet my academic training has been as much in European theory and philosophy as Chinese studies.

When I first began to study Chinese in the United States in the mid-eighties, the People's Republic of China was a poor agrarian country, just beginning to experiment with the decollectivization of agriculture. In elite American universities, Chinese language classes were dwarfed by Japanese ones. While I headed to Taipei and Hong Kong after graduation, most aspiring young people flocked to Tokyo, keen to get in on Japan's spectacular economic rise, driven by a booming stock market and skyrocketing real estate prices. Indeed, everyone's worry at the time was that Japan would simply "buy" America with all the cash it was said to be hoarding. But one of the things that happens as you age is that you get to witness historical change in real time. The Japanese juggernaut stalled as spectacularly as it had risen, while China's subsequent economic takeoff has been world-historic.

This book began as an attempt to try to understand, if only for myself, some of these global transformations I have witnessed in my lifetime. In this sense, it is an extension of inquiries that have preoccupied me for the better part of the past four decades. That makes it also different in style from the bulk of my prior work. Like most academics, my usual procedure is to demonstrate that things are more complicated than they appear, and to reveal hidden politics and histories that remain invisible to an untrained eye. Here, I take the opposite approach. I begin with a subject that everyone agrees is enormously complex—some claim it defies comprehension—and I seek to render it into terms that are accessible and intelligible.

The challenge is to generalize without oversimplifying. This reorientation has required a great deal of self-discipline as well as a move beyond disciplinarity. On the one hand, I have had to rein in my tendency to dwell on details and to dive deeper. On the other hand, this book is less disciplinarily identifiable than my prior work. It is driven by the questions it asks rather than methodological investments. Because I am trying to explicate transformations I have personally seen up close—at least in part—some of what follows might even qualify as participant observation. Most importantly, it draws on a lifetime of learning, reading, and thinking about China and its evolving role in the world. Because the basic ideas of this book have developed over a long period of time, none of them can be traced to a single point of origin. Accordingly, the scholarly apparatus supporting the text is minimal, with references generally only used for direct quotations and statistics. The bibliography lists some key works beyond the ones identified in footnotes that have guided my study, but it is far from comprehensive.

While generalization is necessary, it is also hazardous. The decision to turn to comparative analysis in broadly historical terms thus fills me with some apprehension. By definition, every generalization can be impeached with counterevidence. To borrow Gayatri Spivak's artful observation, "Culture alive is always its irreducible counter-example." Yet our global moment and the shrinking time horizon facing humanity demand macro analyses. Academic specialization has many virtues, but it has costs too. We need both depth and breadth. With the proliferation of subdisciplines, our vertical knowledge of numerous fields has grown immensely. At the same time, though, we are at risk of losing the ability to make horizontal connections across disciplines, time, and space. What I offer here may be in certain ways akin to the kind of grand, big-picture comparative history that was last in vogue in the mid-twentieth century, but I hope to repurpose those projects to meet the demands of the twenty-first century as we are rapidly approaching the natural limits of capitalism.

Brooklyn, NY
October 2025

Introduction
Commodifying Humans and Nature

The law locks up the man or woman
Who steals the goose from off the common,
But leaves the greater villain loose
Who steals the common from the goose.

—"The Goose and the Common"
(undated English poem, nineteenth century)

The Unmaking of the Chinese Working Class offers a structural account of the remarkable political and economic changes that have taken place in the People's Republic of China (PRC) from 1949 to the present as well as an analysis of its role in the global transformations of socialism and capitalism. My title is a deliberate nod to E. P. Thompson's *The Making of the English Working Class.* Thompson's classic study captured vividly the emergence of a working-class consciousness in England, especially during the crucial years between 1780 and 1832, even as he placed his narrative in a much longer history. The English working class constituted the paradigmatic proletariat in the initial stages of industrial capitalism in the West. It is an ideal lens for examining the emergence of another proletariat of global significance on the opposite edge of the Eurasian landmass, one that is emblematic of late-stage capitalism: the Chinese working class.

The ultimate motivation for this study is to gain a better analytic understanding of how capitalism and socialism have developed over the course of the twentieth and twenty-first centuries and the complex ways in which they have been articulated with one another. After the end of the Cold War, capitalism's triumph has come to be seen as inevitable. The transformation of the People's Republic of China into a global superpower has in turn been interpreted largely as evidence of capitalism's superiority as an engine of development. The following pages challenge both views. To state the argument in its most succinct form, China has succeeded economically in many ways not despite but because of its communist legacy. Paradoxically, its global rise is a story of both the unmaking of its working class and of how communism built a capitalist superpower.

As a consequence of its central role in the world economy today, China's significance extends far beyond its borders. In the final analysis, this book is concerned not only with the limitations of global capitalism but with the global limits of economic development tout court, whether pursued in the name of capitalism or socialism. While England's working class paved the way for early industrial capitalism, with China's recent transformation into an economic superpower we are reaching development's natural limits. But in order to imagine and enact an alternative before it is too late, we must first understand how we arrived at this point.

How, then, does the experience of the English working class help us make sense of the present moment? While Thompson's main focus was on the evolving class consciousness of the English worker, he framed his analysis in terms of the Enclosure Movement, dating to the late fifteenth century, which dispossessed peasants of their land and left them with no option but to sell their labor. In China, too, there is occurring a dispossession of peasantry that is often referred to as a New Enclosure Movement (*xin quandi yundong*). In the legal scholar Chun Peng's observation, the scale of rural land takings in China today is "unprecedented in human history."[1] Just between 1990 and 2008—even before the movement's subsequent acceleration—an estimated 88 million peasants had lost their land for development, joining a rapidly expanding population known as "land-losing peasants" (*shidi nongmin*). According to a more recent study,

1 Chun Peng, *Rural Land Takings Law in Modern China: Origin and Revolution* (Cambridge: Cambridge University Press, 2018), 3.

the population of Chinese smallholders has declined by over 200 million since 2001—a loss of household-based land ownership that this study also characterizes as "probably the largest in human history."[2]

Yet the two enclosure movements differ notably in their temporal and spatial scope. Processes that took place over several centuries in England are being telescoped into a few decades in China. What is more, they are taking place in the opposite order: The initial commodification of industrial labor in the 1990s that gave rise to China's gleaming skylines was accompanied by a seemingly inexhaustible stream of migrant laborers into cities even without large-scale commodification of rural land. Why, then, dispossess a peasantry that has already submitted to capital voluntarily—that is, under economic duress without the need to resort to forcible dislocation? The answer to this question turns on the reorganization of the relationship between city and country within China as well as the rearticulation of China's relationship to global capitalism.

When China embarked on its ongoing economic reforms in 1978, it was one of the most equal countries in the world. Today it is one of most unequal ones, as measured by the Gini Index for economic inequality.[3] The changing fortunes of the Chinese working class are a crucial part of this revolution—or, more properly, counterrevolution—as the Chinese Communist Party (CCP) has chosen economic development over equality as its overriding goal.

Importantly, both the making and unmaking of the Chinese working class have unfolded in tandem with the making and unmaking of the Chinese peasantry. Karl Marx believed that communism would lead to the abolition of the distinction between city and country.[4] However, both

---

2 Qian Forrest Zhang and Meiling Wu, "The Decline and Transformation of Smallholders in Chinese Agriculture: National Trends," *Journal of Peasant Studies* 52, no. 3 (2015): 485.

3 Lin Chun, *Revolution and Counterrevolution in China* (London: Verso Books, 2021), 292.

4 Karl Marx and Friedrich Engels, *The Communist Manifesto* (New York: Penguin Books, 2006), 33.

the socialist industry under Mao Zedong and China's booming megalopolises today have been built on the foundation of an impoverished hinterland. It is the peasant's and the urban worker's differentiated relationship to land and labor that has allowed the state to direct a continuous flow of rural resources to cities, first to support industrial labor under state socialism and then to subsidize global capital after China's turn to state capitalism in the 1990s. The changing nature of that relationship is vital for understanding China's astonishing, and astonishingly speedy, transformation as well as its global consequences.

There are numerous excellent studies investigating different aspects of China's development. However, most of them focus on either urban or rural China, or even worse, treat urban institutions as if they represented China as a whole. In order to understand the changing fortunes of the Chinese working class, it is imperative to consider city and country dynamically in relation to one another. Similarly, most analyses of China's political economy focus on either capital or labor. Especially in China's socialist context, the reorganization of capital and the restructuring of labor cannot be grasped unless they are considered as part of a single transformation, with implications not only for the economy but also for the organization of society and family more generally. Furthermore, conventional disciplinary definitions of what *counts* as an economic, political, or social phenomenon are often inadequate for apprehending the Chinese context.

But what follows isn't just a historical account—although that alone would be a significant contribution, given the velocity of change in China over the past decades and how difficult it is even for specialists to develop a big picture view. *The Unmaking of the Chinese Working Class* also situates China's post-1949 political economy within a global perspective. From their very inception, Chinese nationalism and Chinese socialism have been responses to the worldwide expansion of imperialism and capitalism.

Beyond its global framing, this book's analysis is also explicitly comparative, with special attention to the English experience and, to a somewhat lesser degree, to the Soviet one. This comparative angle challenges two dominant narratives of development, both the classical account and a more recent postsocialist one. According to Adam Smith as well as Karl Marx, history proceeds by stages. Both thinkers viewed the Enclosure Movement in England as the classic example of the transition from feudalism to capitalism—with the distinction that Marx thought it would ultimately be followed by socialism. While the Bolshevik Revolution evidently failed to conform to Marx's schema, leapfrogging from feudalism directly to socialism, the dismantling of the Soviet Union in the 1990s has come to be seen as the paradigmatic instance of a socialist transition to capitalism. Much of what we encounter in China will in fact seem similar to both England's passage from feudalism to capitalism and the Soviet Union's postsocialist transition, yet China's experience diverges from both in significant ways.

The value of elaborating comparative counterpoints is not to exceptionalize China, nor to provide yet another account of "capitalism (or socialism) with Chinese characteristics." I take it as a given that there is no capitalism as such: It is always vernacularized in distinctive ways that are specific to time and place, and in China's case its capitalist transformation simply cannot be understood without reference to its communist past and the ongoing effects of that past. But rather than focusing exclusively on China's internal evolution, I wish to analyze it here as a capitalism with global characteristics as well.

The import of historical comparison is heuristic, helping us reconsider some of the key categories by which we have come to narrate the story of China's transformation. Just as Marxian analyses can help us understand China, China can help us rethink Marx and the limits of development. This book employs capitalism and socialism as analytic categories rather than historically reified modes of production. Accordingly, they can be combined and recombined in multiple ways. In this respect, the book's method is indebted to the African American studies scholar Cedric Robinson, who identifies profound continuities between feudalism and contemporary racial capitalism, for example, thus unsettling received Marxian categories.[5]

5 Cedric Robinson, *An Anthropology of Marxism* (Chapel Hill: University of North Carolina Press, 2019).

Indeed, the People's Republic of China displays characteristics that can be classified as socialist, capitalist, and feudal all at once, and indeed Confucian too. To anticipate the story that follows, unlike England, China did not need agrarian capitalism nor a concomitant dispossession of the peasantry as a springboard for its industrial development. Rather, precisely because it has been built on a communist foundation, China's economic success continues to be subsidized by a set of surviving socialist legacies, many of which are in turn embedded in kinship institutions dating from China's imperial past. What is more, because of China's central position in the global manufacturing economy, the socialist subsidy accrues to market actors around the world, allowing consumers everywhere to consume more, and more cheaply, than we otherwise could, thus accelerating the rate at which we damage the very environment that supports us. Hence, China's story should be of interest to anyone concerned about the global present, and indeed about the history as well as the future of the planet.

The English comparison in particular helps us recognize the critical role played by the distinctive forms of public ownership of rural and urban land in the PRC. It is a key premise of this book that there has never been a single People's Republic of China. There have always been (at least) two peoples, if not quite two republics.[6] Ever since agriculture

6 While the distinction between rural and urban forms of public ownership of land is protean, there are evidently numerous other cleavages. Notably, there are male and female citizens—another major categorization that is at once legal and social. There are also multiple ethnic groups with associated legal, social, and cultural distinctions. Likewise, some citizens are politically privileged. All of these distinctions matter, and I attend to them as well as I can, but I focus on the rural-urban divide, especially as it is a less familiar hierarchy to observers outside China. On legalized hierarchies, see Yu Xinzhong, "Citizenship, Ideology, and the PRC Constitution," in Merle Goldman and Elizabeth Perry, eds., *The Changing Meaning of Citizenship in Modern China* (Cambridge, MA: Harvard University Press, 2002), 289–307.

was collectivized following the Land Reform in the early 1950s, every piece of land and every human being in China have been categorized legally and administratively as either urban or rural. Unlike its socialist peers, China never expropriated its peasantry by nationalizing the ownership of *all* land. Even today it distinguishes between two different forms of public ownership: urban land owned by the state and rural land owned by the collectives that cultivate it.

Allowing peasants to remain owners of the land they farmed provided an ideological justification for making them responsible for their subsistence as well as their own welfare needs. At the same time, China turned to the Soviet model for establishing an indigenous heavy industry. Lacking access to external capital, the state began to extract resources from the countryside to set up elite production units in cities which took the form of state-owned enterprises (SOEs). In my nomenclature, this was the original *making* of the Chinese working class—with a crucial difference. The English working class represented a subordinated industrial proletariat, whereas the labor force in SOEs constituted a favored class, a kind of socialist labor aristocracy. Unlike peasants, urban SOE workers enjoyed lifelong job security with cradle-to-grave welfare, funded by the countryside.

To keep peasants—literally—in their place, the PRC enacted a strict household registration (*hukou*) system in 1955. This was essentially a legally enforced caste system that tied a range of state-conferred benefits to residence, ranging from food rations to schooling to medical care. Under this regime of rural-urban segregation, to be categorized a "peasant" (*nongmin*), as opposed to a city-dwelling "worker" (*gongren*), was not only to carry a social label but also to occupy a legally enforced administrative status. Critically, once established, one's residence was virtually untransferable, and it passed down to one's offspring matrilineally, transforming rural poverty into an inherited condition. In contrast to England, the foundation for industrialization was laid not by expropriating peasants of their land but by *tying them to it*. In effect, what had been a smallholding peasantry was feudalized—the very opposite of what happened in England.

This book begins by outlining the English experience and then turns to examining the processes by which land and labor have been commodified in China and their global implications for consumers everywhere, and indeed the globe itself. Below, I first consider why a focus on land and labor is an especially useful way to understand China's transformation as well as the limits of a Marxian analysis of their relationship to one another. Next, I review briefly the original English Enclosure Movement and preview the book's argument about the New Enclosure Movement in China. At this moment of environmental precarity, substituting socialist development for capitalist development is not enough. We must reckon with the global limits not just of capitalism but of economic development in general, at least as we presently conceive it.

Labor and Land

Thompson's ambition was to capture the emergence of a new consciousness among English workers, utilizing all the tools of one of the finest social historians of the twentieth century. With respect to China, such an analysis would be premature. Although there is no doubt that there exists today a Chinese working class in an objective sense, it has not yet acquired a political self-consciousness of the kind described by Thompson. Although it does not lack self-awareness, that self-awareness struggles to find public expression that would allow it to solidify into a political identity. If and when it does, it will have momentous consequences. For now, however, workers have remained mostly too isolated from each other for a collective consciousness to congeal and take an overtly political form—perhaps analogous to the condition of the French peasantry analyzed by Marx in *The Eighteenth Brumaire of Louis Bonaparte*.

My primary aim is thus not to map the subjective experience of Chinese workers, although I pay attention to it where it is relevant and accessible. Rather, I seek to describe analytically the historical, social, political, and economic forces that have coalesced to form the Chinese working class today. I focus on the commodification of land and labor for two reasons. First, a relatively limited focus is necessary to bring analytic clarity to developments whose complexity can be overwhelming. Second, China's relationship to the global economy has been structured to a very large extent by the processes of the commodification of land and labor.

The significance of land and labor is attested to by their extraordinary political sensitivity, often framed as "the Land Question" and "the Peasant Question." Ever since the Tiananmen Square protests in 1989, there is nothing the CCP fears more than the slightest sign of social instability. Most of the reported unrest that has taken place since then has been occasioned not by dissidents calling for greater political participation but by workers objecting to labor conditions and peasants protesting the expropriation of their land. Land and labor matter conceptually *and* politically, and in China's ongoing reforms they are deeply interconnected, much as the Enclosure Movement entailed a profound transformation in the English subjects' relationship to both land and labor.

Let us begin with Marx's views about land and labor. His critique of alienated labor is a full-throated indictment of the exploitation of labor under capitalism. That critique is powerful and familiar. I will not elaborate on it here. Instead, I turn to an important limitation of Marx's analysis. Its signal concern is with the *exploitation of man* by man. In contrast, it takes the *exploitation of nature* by man as a given—indeed, natural.[7] For Marx, the problem with capitalism is not the need to work as such—labor is "the universal condition for the metabolic interaction between man and nature" and hence "common to all forms of society in which

7 There is a great deal of debate whether Marx's understanding of labor as man's mastery over nature constitutes a "Promethean" faith in the power of industrial development or whether his oeuvre also contains the tools for an ecological critique of the natural limits of capitalism. I am sympathetic to the latter view, but as a general matter this ecological debate does not problematize Marx's definition of labor as such, beyond a capitalist context. See, for example, John Bellamy Foster, *Marx's Ecology: Materialism and Nature* (New York: Monthly Review Press, 2000); and Kohei Saito, *Capital, Nature, and the Unfinished Critique of Political Economy* (New York: Monthly Review Press, 2017).

human beings live"—but rather the specific way in which it is organized.[8] Like classical political economists, and Aristotle before them, Marx distinguishes between use value and exchange value: The former is produced for subsistence, or bartered for other useful things, while the latter is exchanged for gain. Offering a universal definition of labor, he characterizes it as purposeful human activity that produces a use value.

Under capitalism, we are conditioned to think about work as a preeminently *social relationship*: one person working for another. However, in the universal sense in which Marx defines it—rather than in the commodified form it takes under capitalism—labor is an expression of *man's relationship to nature*:

> Labour is, first of all, a process between man and nature, a process by which man, through his own actions, mediates, regulates, and controls the metabolism between himself and nature. He confronts the materials of nature as a force of nature. He sets in motion the natural forces which belong to his own body, his arms, legs, head, and hands, in order to appropriate the materials of nature in a form adapted to his own needs.[9]

Specifically, then, labor refers to the interaction between man and land whereby man transforms the latter for his use, or as Marx puts it, soil is "the universal material for human labour."[10]

While all life exists in nature, the way in which the human animal extracts use value from it is unique to him. To be sure, Marx takes pains to acknowledge the remarkable ways in which spiders weave webs and bees construct hives, for example, but he declines categorically to attach the label "work" to such activity, excluding from consideration "instinctive forms of labour which remain on the animal level." What makes labor specifically human is its purposeful nature. While "a bee would put

8 Karl Marx, *Capital*, vol. 1 (New York: Vintage Books, 1977), 290.

9 Ibid., 283.

10 Ibid., 284.

many a human architect to shame by the construction of its honeycomb cells," the architect, unlike the bee, "builds the cell *in his mind* before he constructs it in wax." Rather than merely "instinctive," labor is ultimately creative, setting man apart from nature: "Through this movement he acts upon external nature and changes it, and in this way he simultaneously changes his own nature."[11]

In effect, labor sets man not only apart from but also above nature. Marx characterizes man's exploitation of soil mostly in relatively benign terms as man's "use" of nature, but he also states that the worker "*controls* the metabolism between himself and nature," indeed "*confronts* the materials of nature" in order "to *appropriate*" them. Ultimately, he states, it is a process whereby man "subjects the play of [nature's] forces to his own sovereign power."[12] Friedrich Engels is even more straightforward about the hierarchical relationship between man and nature: "The animal merely *uses* its environment, and brings about changes in it simply by its presence; man by his changes makes it serve his ends, *masters* it."[13] The relationship is ultimately one of subordination rather than mere use.

In short, it is the subjugation of nature that makes us human, forming a vital part of our species-being (*Gattungswesen*). In this regard, Marx is a classical humanist. Significantly, Adam Smith locates man's humanity not in how he makes *use* of the natural environment but in his propensity to *exchange*—a propensity to "truck" and "barter" that is not, he claims, shared by other animals.[14] Because Smith privileges exchange value over use value, for him work is work, whether performed by man or animal: "Not only [the farmer's] labouring servants, but his labouring cattle, are

11 Ibid., 283 (emphasis added).

12 Ibid.

13 Friedrich Engels, "The Part Played by Labor in the Transition from Ape to Man," in *The Origin of the Family, Private Property, and State* (New York: International Publishers, 1972), 260 (emphasis in original).

14 Adam Smith, *An Inquiry into the Nature and Causes of the Wealth of Nations—A Selected Edition* (Oxford: Oxford University Press, 1993), bk. I, ch. 2, 21.

productive labourers."[15] Rather than the locus of a worker's humanity, laboring is an expression of his animality. Accordingly, for Smith the profit-seeking capitalist is the apotheosis of the human, whereas for Marx it is the worker.

Yet to the extent that the Enclosure Movement entailed the commodification of land as well as labor, it had consequences well beyond human life. In the analysis of the economic historian Karl Polanyi, these twinned processes played a key role in Europe's transformation into what he calls "market society" in the eighteenth and nineteenth centuries. In Polanyi's view, they far outranked the significance of commodity markets, which he did not consider an especially distinctive phenomenon: They have been present in many different types of societies. What is significant about markets for labor and land is that they aren't products themselves but factors of production—means by which goods are produced.[16]

More specifically, Polanyi calls land and labor "fictitious commodities" in recognition of the fact that they are not produced *for markets*. Evidently, land is not produced at all: It preexists markets, nor can we produce any more of it than already exists, since even the reclamation of land has finite limits. To be sure, even under capitalism workers are—and must be—continually produced and reproduced, but not for the purely instrumental purpose of satisfying labor markets (in contrast to, say, slave societies). Effectively, Polanyi argues, the commodification of labor amounts to a *commodification of humans*, while the commodification of land represents nothing less than a *commodification of nature*. The problem, therefore, with the commodification of land is not only that, historically, it entails the expropriation of the peasant but that it alters our relationship to the environment in which we exist—indeed, the environment in which all life on this planet exists. Stated differently, that environment *is* life itself.

15 Ibid., bk. II, ch. 5, 217.

16 See Karl Polanyi, *The Great Transformation: The Political and Economic Origins of Our Time* (Boston, MA: Beacon Press, 1957).

It should not surprise us, then, that in China, too, the commodification of humans and the commodification of nature have been especially contentious processes. Given their interconnected nature, the Enclosure Movement provides an especially apt historical and analytic frame for considering the transformations of the Chinese working class and its crucial significance for the development of global capitalism.[17]

The English Enclosure Movement

Until the late fifteenth and early sixteenth century, English farming was conducted largely in manorial estates organized as common fields. This was a system of subsistence agriculture with overlapping individual and collective elements. Tenants of various kinds possessed strips of land they held individually, but fields were worked both individually and collectively. There were also additional village lands subject to collective use, encompassing a wide range of customary rights, many of which were available to landless commoners as well:

17 The relative inattention to the Enclosure Movement in England in analyzing rural China today is as much a Chinese as Western phenomenon, although in China's case the reasons are increasingly political. The agricultural economist Wen Tiejun began to note parallels between the Enclosure Movement in England and China's contemporary development as early as the 1990s and early 2000s. See, for example, Wen Tiejun and Zhu Shouyin, "Zhengfu Ziben Yuanshi Jilei yu Tudi Nong Zhuan Fei [Primitive Accumulation of Government Capital and the Conversion of Agricultural Land to Non-Agricultural Uses]," *Jingli Shijie* [Management World] 5 (2006): 161–6. However, especially after the rise of Xi Jinping making such references has become increasingly sensitive politically. In the sociologist Zhang Yulin's estimation, by 2015 the use of the term "Enclosure Movement"—even in quotation marks—had come to be seen as a "provocation." Zhang Yulin, "Da Qingchang: Zhongguo de Quandi Yundong ji qi yu Zhongguo de Bijiao [The Great Clearance: The Enclosure Movement in China and Its Comparison with England]," *Zhongguo Nongyue Dazue Xuebao (Shehui Kexue Ban)* [Journal of China Agricultural University (Social Science Edition)] 32, no. 1 (2015): 19–45.

pasturing domestic animals, gathering firewood, cutting peat, and so on.

Markets for agricultural products grew over time, and with accelerating rates of urbanization their prices rose accordingly—first for wool and soon for grain. To produce for sale, lords began to expel their tenants and to enclose the commons. This was part of an uneven pattern that marked the breakup of agricultural land across Europe. Enclosure was accomplished through legal measures as well as extralegal violence, transforming lands encumbered with customary rights and overlapping tenures into exclusive forms of modern property that could be bought and sold at will by a singular owner. For Marx, these initial acts of violence and dispossession constituted the paradigmatic instance of "primitive accumulation," or "an accumulation not the result of the capitalist mode of production but its point of departure."[18]

With a shift from feudal subsistence farming to agrarian capitalism, growing rural capital in turn provided the foundation for new forms of industry, starting with textile mills and rural manufactures and culminating eventually in urban industries. Once the commons were enclosed and their occupants expropriated, the erstwhile peasants had nothing left to sell but their labor. It was thus their *alienation from land* that gave them no choice but to take on *alienated labor* and, accordingly, they became the original working class whose coming to self-consciousness Thompson investigates. The commodification of land and labor were thus overlapping historical processes, with the former laying the foundation for the latter. Insofar as there were nonetheless "sturdy rogues" and other lazy folk who preferred a life of vagabondage and chose to live by begging or hunting, for example, the Parliament enacted a body of what Marx called "Bloody Legislation against the Expropriated" that outlawed loitering as well as beggary. The privatization of the commons was accompanied by the enclosure of England's royal forests—a vital source of subsistence for many—and a concurrent

18 Marx, *Capital*, vol. 1, 873.

criminalization of fishing and hunting, turning living off of nature into "poaching" punishable by death.[19]

While Marx accorded a central role to the Enclosure Movement as an engine of capitalism's development in England, he recognized the global reach of primitive accumulation, with imperial dominions providing resources, labor, and captive markets for English goods—say, American plantations delivering cotton for the mills in England where it was transformed into textiles that were then exported to India, ultimately decimating local producers. Indeed, because the Enclosure Movement coincided with the rise of colonialism, the new regime of land ownership was eventually exported to wherever colonists chose to settle, displacing indigenous relationships between humans and nature. By way of analogy, we can think of the concurrent rise of the nation-state as a political enclosure movement, one that has turned the entire planet into a juridical formation made up of states with exclusive control over their territories. With coastal states making claims over the seabed and what has historically been recognized as the free seas, many are speaking of the enclosure of the oceans as well. Others in turn have characterized the establishment of intellectual property as the privatization of our intellectual commons.

With respect to England, views on the significance of the Enclosure Movement diverge depending largely on whether one focuses on its economic or political consequences. Even while acknowledging the movement's extraordinary violence, the sociologist Barrington Moore Jr., for example, is concerned primarily with its political legacy. In *Social Origins of Dictatorship and Democracy: Lord and Peasant in the Making of the Modern World*, he celebrates the peasant's expropriation as his emancipation: Freed from feudal subjection, he became politically independent, laying the foundation for modern democratic citizenship. Marx hardly bemoans the disappearance of feudal hierarchies, but his focus is

19 See "Chapter 28: Bloody Legislation Against the Expropriated," in ibid., 896–904; Charles R. Young, *The Royal Forests of Medieval England* (Philadelphia: University of Pennsylvania Press, 1979); and E. P. Thompson, *Whigs and Hunters: The Origin of the Black Act* (London: Allen Lane, 1975).

overwhelmingly on the novel forms of economic subjection rather than on political liberation, which he finds illusory.

In China, too, there is occurring a dispossession of peasantry that entails the commodification of land and labor, with major political and economic consequences. Although the privatization of various types of collectively held land and the associated destruction of customary rights have been a common feature in the geographic expansion of capitalist relations everywhere, they have taken notably dramatic and brutal forms in England and China.

The Chinese Enclosure Movement

It is a well-known though often already forgotten fact that China's post-Mao economic transformation began in the countryside with agricultural reforms followed by rural industrialization. It was the astonishing growth of rural enterprise from the 1980s through the mid-1990s that lifted millions of peasants out of poverty and drove China's unprecedented expansion during this period. In a striking reversal, in subsequent years the countryside has stagnated while urban centers have far outpaced it, with shimmering megacities becoming the horizon of the new millennium. Yet for the first two decades of the reform era, when outside observers referred to the Chinese economic miracle, what they were really talking about was a *rural* industrial revolution, not the Chinese economy as a whole.

When the economic reforms began in 1978, their primary focus was on the alleviation of rural poverty. Each household was allocated a temporary use right for a small plot along with the right to sell whatever it produced above its assigned quota. Although rural land remained collectively owned, this relatively circumscribed reform gave rise to a limited market for agricultural commodities. At the same time, there arose a new wave of rural industry that came to be organized in the form of rural collectives, known as Township and Village Enterprises (TVEs).

In some ways, this was similar to the English experience. There, too, industry emerged early on in the countryside, supplementing agriculture without displacing it. In the Chinese case, however, peasants *owned* the land and the capital, and evidently, they did not need to dispossess themselves in order to operate their own enterprises. TVEs' stunning success is often attributed to an incipient "liberalization" of the economy, as if they represented a spontaneous incarnation of the spirit of capitalism emanating from Chinese soil. However, this book argues that the early rural reforms ought to be viewed as an instance of *socialist* development: An autochthonous form of local public enterprise, TVEs represented the transformation of what had been an agricultural commons into an industrial one.

TVEs' economic rise in the 1980s and through the early 1990s quickly began to close the welfare gap between peasants and their urban compatriots. At the same time, it redoubled the pressure on the increasingly beleaguered urban state sector. In the mid-1990s the state made a decisive turn from rural to urban reform, in favor of industrial state capitalism over collectivized rural industry. It is this state capitalism and the stunning skylines it has built that represent China in the global media today.

The state initiated the process by restructuring its legal relationship to both capital and labor. With the aid of a new Company Law that came into effect in 1994, SOEs were transformed into the legal form of the corporation. While the state remained the controlling shareholder, it began to invite global capital to help turn its SOEs into profit-making corporations. With respect to labor, SOE workers owned no land. Instead, they were dispossessed of their primary socialist entitlement: lifetime job security. It was this commodification of labor—known colloquially as "breaking the iron rice bowl"—that constituted the *unmaking* of the Chinese working class as a privileged socialist stratum, inaugurating its transformation into a run-of-the-mill industrial proletariat of the kind described by Thompson.

However, especially after China joined the World Trade Organization (WTO) in 2001, its cities were flooded with global capital, and the existing urban labor force was no longer sufficient. At the same time, rural China was awash with unemployed and underemployed peasants. This gave rise to a growing tide of migrant labor flowing from the countryside to cities. The dismantling of SOEs was in turn accompanied by the commodification of urban land for housing and private development—a process that has culminated in a massive real estate bubble that threatens the Chinese economy today. Importantly, after accommodations and other necessities became available through markets, peasants have been able to move to cities even without an urban registration. Yet they remain second-class citizens without access to the full range of benefits available to registered urban residents. Accordingly, they shuttle back and forth between their jobs and their villages, relying on the land their families continue to till for subsistence when they lose their jobs, do not get paid, or become injured.

The key to China's proverbially "cheap" labor lies in this hybrid character of its migrant workers. Under socialism, the state extracted the product of peasants' labor. Today urban capital extracts the ablest peasants themselves, albeit only temporarily and on a rotational basis while they continue to be supported by their villages as well. Migrant workers are effectively a reserve army of commodified labor that bears the costs of its own reproduction—not unlike undocumented immigrants in the United States, for example. It is these workers' ongoing reliance on the support of their rural kin that makes it possible for urban employers to pay them cut-rate wages. The question is therefore not how these migrants have been able to *avoid* expropriation, in contrast to the early English industrial proletariat. Rather, it is precisely their continuing ownership of land—possibly the single most important achievement of the Chinese Revolution—that allows today's state capitalism to exploit them.

After the initial commodification of urban land in the 1990s, the enclosure of rural land consisted primarily in the absorption of peri-urban villages into adjoining cities. In contrast, the current wave of enclosures is aimed at transforming rural China itself. The state's goal is to consolidate agricultural land into large industrial farms and to relocate the displaced peasants in cities, including "New Cities" (*xincheng*) built specifically for that purpose. To accomplish this, rural land itself is being finally commodified: Members of rural collectives are now permitted to transfer the right to use their land to outsiders, including representatives of agribusiness. (Formally, households are only allowed to lease the right to *use* their plots—subject to some approvals and land-use restrictions—rather than the plots "themselves," which allows the Party to continue to state that all land remains publicly owned.) Accordingly, the consolidation of household land into industrial farms takes the form of voluntary market transactions, yet in practice those transactions are often coercive, "facilitated" by the intermediation of officials. With the arrival of agribusiness, the countryside, too, is becoming integrated into Chinese state capitalism, no longer its rural other.

After joining the WTO, China has had no shortage of either capital or labor—the former flows in from global markets, the latter from the countryside. To sustain its economic growth, what China needs most today is *markets*, including markets for its products at home. The problem with migrant labor is that its proletarianization remains partial. It depends on capital for wages, but so long as it is able to fall back on subsistence agriculture it does not depend on wages *exclusively*. Moreover, not only do peasants remain at least partly independent of markets, but because of their economic and social precarity, they save every penny they can, thus consuming even less than they would otherwise. Stated differently, they make first-rate workers and second-rate consumers. The commodification of industrial labor has already transformed them into a reserve army of labor. The recent commodification of rural land holds the promise of turning them into a reserve army of consumers as well: Fully dependent on capital for survival, they will be left with no choice but to buy everything they need. In effect, *the enclosure of China's countryside completes the proletarianization of the peasantry*.

Marx characterized primitive accumulation as the economic equivalent of the theological idea of "original sin."[20] In contrast to Marx, the Polish German revolutionary socialist Rosa Luxemburg insisted that even mature capitalism cannot produce surplus value out of nothing—it is not

20 Marx, *Capital*, vol. 1, 873.

a system of alchemy, after all. To be able to reproduce itself over time, capitalism must engage in a continual process of primitive accumulation, for which it always needs an unequal outside from which to draw resources.[21] As the New Enclosure Movement is proceeding, it is striking that Chinese capital—both state and private capital—is increasingly looking for outlets elsewhere, such as resource extraction projects in Africa. With the recent Belt and Road Initiative, China is spreading its investments even more widely. Running out of lands to enclose and people to dispossess at home, Chinese capital, too, is going global, setting up Sinocentric production chains ranging from the Indian Ocean to Latin America. Thus, we are left with the question: What are the planetary limits of capitalism? This takes us back to Homo sapiens' troubled relationship with nature.

This book outlines the rise and fall of the Chinese working class in light of its communist history and what the nation's concomitant transformation into an economic superpower means for the future of capitalism and the world. All the essential elements in this story are known, but they sit in separate disciplinary silos, making it difficult to grasp them in their totality. The following chapters organize them into a single structural account, one with a historical narrative as well as an analytic framework. Without such a framework, we cannot apprehend late-stage capitalism and China's central role in its transformation with the critical urgency and moral clarity they demand. Perhaps a more sober understanding will allow us to rethink our relationship to labor and land, production and nature, and ultimately the future of the planet on which we travel through space and time.

---

21 See generally Rosa Luxemburg, *The Accumulation of Capital* (New Haven, CT: Yale University Press, 1951).

1

Making Workers and Peasants: Socialist Foundations, 1949–1978

Man can be reformed!

—Mao Zedong

Global capitalism today simply could not function as it does without China. To understand how one of the leading socialist states of the world became the economic superpower it is today, we must start with the labor and land regimes of the People's Republic upon its founding.

Marx defined landed property as a monopoly that empowers proprietors to "dispose of particular portions of the globe as exclusive spheres of their private will to the exclusion of all others."[1] Under socialism there will be no need for property, landed or otherwise, and the earth will belong to all. But before socialism is fully achieved, the socialist state represents the interests of the people. The nationalization of land is literally the foundation of a socialist state: It forms the very ground on which the state is erected. In China, too, the Communist Party's moral authority lies in its stewardship of the "sacred territory" it occupies, in the language of the PRC Constitution.[2] Significantly, however, all land in China does *not* fall under state ownership. Instead, the PRC differentiates between two species of what it calls "public property,"

1 Karl Marx, *Capital*, vol. 3 (London: Penguin Classics, 1981), 752.

2 Constitution of the People's Republic of China [*Zhonghua Renmin Gongheguo Xianfa*], Preamble (stating that Taiwan is part of "the sacred territory of the People's Republic of China").

depending on whether the property in question is urban or rural. Only land that is classified legally as urban is owned by the state. In contrast, rural land is owned not by the state but by the collective organizations that cultivate and utilize it.[3]

This legal distinction is specific to Chinese socialism. It has no precedent in Marxist theory or praxis, nor is it a vestige of premodern forms of ownership. It is also crucial for understanding the divergent stories of rural and urban China. When juxtaposed to one another, the two seem worlds apart—one defined by stagnation, the other by soaring skylines. In fact, their fates are deeply entwined and they form part of a single narrative: There would be no booming Chinese cities without an exploited hinterland. These two Chinas' distinct land regimes form the literal and figurative foundation of that story. This chapter tells why and how this distinction materialized at the state's founding; how it gave rise to China's two "leading classes," workers and peasants; and how these developments both accorded with and diverged from Marxian thought as well as the experience of both England and the Soviet Union.

Toward the Socialist State

When Mao Zedong stood up on top of the Tiananmen Gate in Beijing on October 1, 1949, and proclaimed the establishment of the People's Republic of China, the Communist Party was faced with a classic sovereignty project. First, it had to erect a new state to govern the territory it controlled. Second, it had to organize the subjects of the new polity. In the political scientist James Scott's phrase, the Party had to create a machinery for "seeing like a state," or making the subject population legible to the bureaucracies that would administer them.[4] Third, to be recognized as a sovereign state, it also had to conform to certain global

3 This generalization holds true for cultivated land and adjacent areas. Mining lands, lakes, and forests not utilized by collectives are owned by the state.

4 James C. Scott, *Seeing Like a State: How Certain Schemes to Improve the Human Condition Have Failed* (New Haven, CT: Yale University Press, 1999).

standards. To paraphrase Scott, it had to *be seen like a state*. By 1949, there was an established script for a socialist polity, set by the Soviet Union—even if many capitalist states refused to recognize its legitimacy—and in general terms, the PRC followed that script. When it came to the specifics of how to organize the people of the People's Republic, however, China ultimately departed from the Soviet precedent, creating its own distinctive regime for organizing its citizens' productivity and controlling their mobility.

At the outset, it is vital to recognize that the notion of a socialist state is itself an oxymoron, despite the fact that as an institution it came to dominate much of the twentieth century. In the Marxian view, the state serves the interests of the ruling class and functions ultimately as its executive committee. With the arrival of socialism, it will become an anachronism and simply wither away, or as Friedrich Engels put it epigrammatically, the state will "end up where it will then belong," namely, "the museum of antiquities, next to the spinning wheel and the bronze ax."[5] Historically, however, socialist regimes have been states on steroids, with an extreme centralization of coercive power.

The reason for this dramatic departure of history from theory—what Marx theorized as the laws of historical materialism—is as simple as it is profound. Marx anticipated a *global* communist revolution. According to *The Communist Manifesto*, "The working men have no country."[6] Marx's revolutionary call is not addressed to the French working class, or the English or the German one. As he elaborates elsewhere, "The nationality of the worker is neither French, nor English, nor German, it is *labor* . . . His government is neither French, nor English, nor German, it is *capital*."[7]

---

5 Friedrich Engels, *The Origin of the Family, Private Property, and the State* (New York: International Publishers, 1972), 232.

6 Karl Marx and Friedrich Engels, *The Communist Manifesto* (New York: Penguin Books, 2006), 29.

7 Karl Marx, "Draft of an Article on Friedrich List's Book *Das nationale System der politischen Ökonomie*," in Karl Marx and Friedrich Engels, *Collected Works*, vol. 4 (Electric Book, 2010), 280 (emphasis in original).

Precisely because capital follows profit without respect for national borders, the communist revolution, too, must be worldwide. Hence the *Manifesto*'s unmistakably global rallying cry: "Working men of all countries, unite!"[8]

As a nineteenth-century intellectual, Marx was influenced by scientism as well as evolutionism. The would-be-scientific laws of historical materialism he put forward predicted not just a world revolution but also that it would take place only after the world had passed through capitalism, the penultimate historical stage. Yet when the Bolsheviks seized power in Russia in October 1917, their revolution defied both predictions. The first successful communist uprising did not take place in England, the home of the latest advances of industrial capitalism, but in one of the most economically backward corners of Europe, a vast agrarian empire whose population consisted mostly of recently emancipated serfs.[9] Nor did the storming of the Winter Palace spark a global revolution. On the contrary, simply taking the revolution from St. Petersburg and Russia's major cities to the rest of the country required several years of civil war and the quelling of numerous peasant revolts.

In the absence of a world revolution, it would have been political suicide for the Bolsheviks to wind down the institutions of the state while surrounded by internal and external adversaries. In anticipation of this, in 1917 Lenin published *The State and Revolution*, which elaborated on Marx's idea of a "dictatorship of the proletariat" as a transitional political

8 Marx and Engels, *The Communist Manifesto*, 52.

9 In the final stages of his career Marx turned his focus away from the European heartland and began to research noncapitalist formations elsewhere. In his posthumously published *Ethnological Notebooks*, he reconsidered his original stadial framework and the possibility that Russia, for example, could simply skip capitalism, with the traditional rural village, *mir*, providing the foundation for a transition to communism. In any event, the outbreak of the Great War in 1914 dashed the dream of a world revolution, proving that workers were more prepared to shed blood in a war against one another than to disavow their national identifications.

form. As the new ruling class, the workers were to own the means of production and to be in charge of the state apparatus. To the extent that Russia's underdeveloped proletariat had not yet reached full self-consciousness and a sufficient level of organization, its interests would be represented by the Communist Party as its vanguard.

Following the conclusion of a bloody civil war and the establishment of the Union of Soviet Socialist Republics (USSR) in 1922, Stalin transformed what Lenin had envisioned as a temporary concession to necessity into a permanent concentration of unrestricted state power, or what he called "socialism in one country": a stand-alone socialist state with a strong military and a powerful industrial base capable of resisting its capitalist enemies. It was this historical and geopolitical conjuncture that gave birth to the distinctive twentieth-century phenomenon of a Communist Party-state.

The "China" and "the People" of the People's Republic of China

In 1949, the People's Republic of China set itself up as a socialist state on the Soviet model. In addition to establishing state organs, it had to organize its population into appropriate political categories. Crucially, the revolution did not simply recognize peasants and workers as the leading classes of the PRC: It made them, and it assigned them spatial coordinates. Ultimately peasants became tied to the land they plowed, while workers in the technical socialist sense were attached to their urban work units. Arriving at this eventual binary arrangement was not straightforward. It began with constructing and ranking a wide range of political subjects according to socialist criteria.

Even the most basic determinations were difficult. What was the "China" of the People's Republic of China and who were the "People" that composed it? How much land and which people(s) would the new state claim? These questions hearkened back to the establishment of the Republic of China (ROC) in 1912. The Qing (1644–1911 CE) had been a multiethnic empire governed by a Manchu dynasty. Sun Yat-sen and many of his revolutionary followers in the South had initially advocated replacing the imperial behemoth with a modern republic that would occupy, and be limited to, the Han Chinese heartland. Yuan Shikai and the Northern warlords promoted a new constitutional monarchy that would hold on to the vast Manchu conquests that had expanded the empire's reach during the mid-Qing period. The new Republic of China became an unstable compromise that sought to have it both ways. It took the political form of a republic yet retained its predecessor's imperial footprint—it was half republic, half empire.

At first it seemed that the PRC would reject the imperial overreach of the ROC. After its founding in 1921, the Chinese Communist Party followed the Soviet party line, which had accorded, at least in principle, the ethnically non-Russian peoples of the czarist empire the right of national self-determination. Hence, the new state was emphatically not "the People's Republic of Russia" but was organized as a Union of Soviet Socialist Republics instead. However, by 1949 Mao Zedong and the CCP had changed their minds, downgrading the non-Han populations of the Qing empire into "minority nationalities" rather than nations with a right of self-determination. Accordingly, the PRC to this day remains heir to the imperial legacy of the Qing. The one thing the PRC and the Nationalists' rump parliament in Taiwan continued to agree on even after 1949 was that China meant *all* of China at its widest imperial extension.

With the matter of the nation's territorial reach thus ideologically settled (even as it remains politically contested to this day), there were further questions about the actual people who made up the new China. In a political sense, the term "people" did not refer to the people of China as a whole but only to those who shared the class and national interests of the Chinese Communist Revolution. Those who did not were categorically not part of the people in a political sense, and to the extent they were opposed to those interests, they were enemies of the people. However, unlike their Russian counterparts, the Chinese communists fought their civil war *before* their revolutionary takeover. When the PRC was formally established, the principal enemies of the people had already been defeated and sent packing to Taiwan, the new "temporary" seat of the Nationalist government under the US-supported Chiang Kai-shek.

With respect to its internal political structure, the new state adopted the Leninist model of a dictatorship of proletariat, or in Mao Zedong's somewhat more inclusive rendering, "the people's democratic dictatorship." The basic principle was the same: democracy to the people and dictatorship to its enemies. The term "proletariat," however, refers to a single class, whereas "the people" in the Maoist sense is a political category consisting of multiple classes, the makeup of which at any time varies according to political circumstances. At its establishment, the PRC was premised on the foundational alliance of workers and peasants, the two privileged classes spearheading the revolution. In addition, the Party acknowledged the patriotic roles played by the petty bourgeoisie and the national bourgeoisie (in contrast to their sell-out counterparts, the comprador capitalists). In recognition of this fact, the four small stars on the PRC flag stand for these four classes.

Mao Zedong's promotion of peasants to a vital revolutionary role represented a new development in socialist theory and practice. The Russian Revolution had followed the Marxist playbook insofar as it was indeed a workers' revolt, one that originated in cities among the country's incipient proletariat. Lenin and most of his comrades had outright contempt for the Russian peasantry, regarding it as benighted and an impediment to the revolution, even while they recognized that they needed its compliance. In this, they largely reproduced the anti-rural bias of Marx himself, who notoriously denounced "the idiocy of rural life" and compared the French peasantry to a sack of potatoes.[10]

The CCP too emerged from an elite setting. Founded in Shanghai in 1921, its membership consisted primarily of urban intellectuals and activists. Under Bolshevik guidance, the CCP at first put aside its ideological differences and cooperated with the Nationalist government in Nanjing, only to be driven out of the areas under Nationalist control when Chiang Kai-shek unleashed his campaign of White Terror in 1927.

10 See Marx and Engels, *The Communist Manifesto*, 9; and Karl Marx, *The Eighteenth Brumaire of Louis Bonaparte* (New York: International Publishers, 1994), 124.

As the Party set out on the legendary Long March, the experience transformed Mao Zedong, a charismatic and strategically gifted villager from Hunan, into the Party's supreme leader. After displacing the Party's Bolshevik faction, Mao nationalized the revolution and turned the CCP from an arm of a Soviet-led international movement into an authentically Chinese one.

What is more, the ensuing years of hiding out in the hinterlands reoriented the Chinese Revolution to the countryside. While Lenin's revolution began in the cities and was then exported to the country—where it faced great resistance—Mao Zedong followed the opposite strategy of using "the countryside to surround the cities." Hence, the Chinese Revolution did not begin with the Chairman climbing to the top of the Tiananmen Gate—the Chinese equivalent of seizing the Winter Palace—but culminated there, signaling not the start but the end of military struggle. From the very beginning, then, the PRC was a union of workers *and* peasants.

Yet this storied alliance was always asymmetrical. In 1951, China's urban proletariat is estimated to have made up less than 1 percent of the country's population.[11] Although peasants were far more numerous and did the bulk of the fighting, their union with workers was led by the latter by virtue of the more advanced class consciousness attributed to them. Even as peasants had been indispensable in establishing a revolutionary China, *they* would now have to be remade to conform to the standards of socialist modernity. Their putative feudal backwardness came to justify the creation of a set of unequal economic structures that laid the foundation for the establishment of an industrial workforce that would help China compete in the rapidly accelerating Cold War.

Let us begin with the workers, the leading class of the new China.

---

11 Felix Wemheuer, *A Social History of Maoist China: Conflict and Change, 1949–1976* (Cambridge: Cambridge University Press 2019), 87.

The Making of the Chinese Working Class

The transformation of socialism into statism was just one consequence of the failure of the Russian Revolution to trigger a worldwide collapse of capitalism. For the sake of ensuring its competitiveness amongst its capitalist enemies, Stalin developed an industrial machine that altered the very goals of socialism, or at least deferred them indefinitely. A theory that originated as a project of universal human emancipation turned into a program of economic development. The establishment of state socialism did not lead to the abolition of property. Rather, it scaled it up by converting everything into the property of the state—a form of super-property.

From this perspective, state socialism's commitment to industrial development can even be described as a kind of state capitalism. Marx himself suggested as much, indicating (critically) that state ownership of capital—or what he called "communal capital"—would turn the community into "a universal capitalist," with the community taking the position of the proprietor and paying wages to those laboring for it.[12] The Soviet Union organized its heavy industry in just this manner, in the form of state-owned enterprises in which the state owned the capital and compensated the workers for their labor.

In this regard, too, the PRC followed the Soviet model. It started by setting up elite industrial divisions structured as SOEs. Each urban resident was assigned to a work unit (*danwei*), which was much more than a production division. A classic SOE constituted a miniature welfare state, providing not only guaranteed lifetime employment—the vaunted "iron rice bowl"—but also a cradle-to-grave system of care and control, including benefits such as housing, childcare, educational, medical, athletic and cultural facilities, and provisions for retirement. As the introduction suggested, this reorganization of the

---

12 Karl Marx, "Private Property and Communism," in *Economic and Philosophic Manuscripts of 1844* (Mineola, NY: Dover Publications, 2004), 100.

urban labor force constituted the original *making* of the Chinese working class, not in the sense of a subordinated industrial proletariat but in the sense of a privileged stratum of socialist citizenry—a socialist aristocracy of sorts.

While SOEs' premises and capital were owned by the state and the workers were employees who were remunerated for their labor by the state, industrial workers were nonetheless officially hailed as "the masters of the factory" (*gongchang de zhuren*). The term "state-owned enterprise" was in fact shorthand for the legal designation "industrial enterprise owned by the whole people" (*quanmin suoyouzhi gongye qiye*). This terminology construed the state's employment of its citizens as one in which the workers were *self*-employed: Since the enterprise was owned by the people and workers were part of the people, they were theoretically working for themselves, not performing alienated labor for an employer. But despite ideological claims to the contrary, in material terms the state was the workers' landlord as well as employer.

It is important to recognize the radical nature of the SOE as an institution, even by comparison to its Soviet counterpart. The work unit in a Chinese SOE was nothing short of a total institution. Architecturally, a typical SOE was structured in the form of a classic four-walled compound—the same configuration as the traditional Chinese house, temple, and palace. Functionally, it combined the operations of the market, the state, and the family in a single entity. Accordingly, it had benign as well as totalitarian aspects. In material terms, workers enjoyed remarkably equal treatment not only with respect to one another but even their superiors. Although all major decisions were made by the Party-state, at lower levels of hierarchy workers also enjoyed genuine workplace democracy, selecting their own supervisors on the factory floor, for example. With no mechanisms of coercion at their disposal, supervisors had little choice but to rely on persuasion. At the same time, however, the work unit was an arm of the state and the main site for the governance, surveillance, and political instruction of the urban citizenry. From a positive vantage point, the system was one of participatory paternalism, while from a negative one it subjected work-unit members to a system of organized dependence on the state.[13]

The abolition of property was not the only socialist goal on which state socialism compromised. With respect to the future of bourgeois kinship, *The Communist Manifesto* was equally unambiguous about its agenda: "Abolition of the family!"[14] The justifications for the abolition of property and family were closely related. To the extent that the latter was a bourgeois institution seeking to hoard property and pass it on from one generation to another, its raison d'être was expected to disappear after the revolution, much like that of the state that protected property in the first place. But just as the PRC eliminated only private property and elevated public property in its stead, it also restrained from abolishing the family and hoped to transform it instead—if not quite into a "public family," ideally at least something approximating it.

In the Confucian ideology of the late imperial Chinese state, ritual kinship had been the social and political essence of a properly governed polity. The Nationalist government had sought to replace the patriarchal Confucian conception with the modern nuclear family, based on a consensual and egalitarian bond between husband and wife, but its efforts found mixed success. Instead, the Communist Party's new ideals envisioned the sublimation of every comrade's libido into a passion for socialism, the motherland, and the Great Helmsman himself. As a matter of realism, however, the PRC acknowledged the continuing appeal of conjugal attachments. In 1950, it passed a Marriage Law that recognized

13 For sociological analyses that focus on the negative aspects of dependence as well as the participatory elements of the work unit's paternalism, respectively, see Andrew Walder, *Communist Neo-Traditionalism: Work and Authority in Chinese Industry* (Berkeley: University of California Press, 1988), and Joel Andreas, *Disenfranchised: The Rise and Fall of Industrial Citizenship in China* (Oxford: Oxford University Press, 2019).

14 Marx and Engels, *The Communist Manifesto*, 27.

the family while seeking to remake the "feudal" (in Marxian parlance) kinship structures that supported it.

Even though the PRC fell short of the full gender equality it promoted in marriage and in society, it raised women's economic and social status to an unprecedented degree. Unlike the Soviet Union with its strongly pro-natalist policies, the PRC did not privilege women's reproductive role above their participation in the workforce. Childcare, for instance, was socialized in SOEs, thus freeing—and obligating—women to work along with men. As Chinese women were brought fully into production and paid for their labor, they acquired a new sense of economic agency and public recognition beyond their domestic roles. To be sure, like their sisters in capitalist economies, Chinese women continued to carry the primary responsibility for domestic labor, receiving compensation only for what was deemed to be "productive labor." Moreover, they earned fewer work points even for the labor for which they were compensated, based on the theory that, as the weaker sex, they were less productive. At the same time, while the socialist work unit did not abolish the family, it made it subject to state planning, much like other aspects of society. Even intimate decisions such as whom to marry required cadre approval, and, with the one-child policy, even family planning became subject to the state plan.

Put simply, the SOE was a total institution that combined economic, political, and familial elements into a single entity, all under the umbrella of state ownership.

The Invention of the Chinese Peasant

While workers were the leading class of the revolution, peasants were their principal ally. The industrial worker was an unimpeachable socialist hero helping advance the PRC into industrial modernity. The peasant, in contrast, is an ambiguous figure, politically a vital confederate yet ideologically always suspect. In Marxian historiography, peasants—no matter how patriotic—represent remnants of the feudal mode of production. One of the main responsibilities of the Chinese Revolution was therefore to remake them. But before he could be remade, the peasant had to be invented.[15]

In the first place, this invention satisfied the demands of socialist theory, but it also served the Party's political purposes, helping justify its strategy of shifting resources from the countryside to SOEs. The Chinese peasant was the material precondition of the socialist worker's existence. When the PRC set out to establish SOEs, the nationalization of existing industries was relatively easy, as the Nationalist government had already taken over the key ones. The ROC was also a Party-state, and over the course of the Sino-Japanese War and its civil war with the Communists it had already taken over the nation's critical industries in order to support the war effort. The PRC was thus able simply to step into its predecessor's shoes and take over extant state-owned enterprises.

But those enterprises were far from enough to advance the PRC to the level of industrial productivity it desired. Although it received some aid from the Soviet Union, especially after joining the Korean War, its access to external funding was limited. Indeed, it found itself in the same position as the Soviet Union had: with an abundance of labor and a scarcity of capital. Here too the PRC followed in the footsteps of its Soviet elder brother. Deliberately delinking from the world economy, it turned to what was effectively a socialist version of an originally capitalist strategy. Marx had

15 See generally Myron L. Cohen, "Cultural and Political Inventions in Modern China: The Case of the Chinese 'Peasant,' " *Dædalus* 122, no. 2 (1993): 151–70. The category of peasant is gender-neutral, yet Chinese socialist feminism's ideology of sameness tends simply to assimilate women to men. Accordingly, I employ the male pronoun in a universal sense when referring to peasants as an ideological construct, in contrast to "actual" male or female peasants. With respect to urban workers, it is of course vital to recognize that in practice they too required molding and were subject to continuous discipline and monitoring, but at least as an ideological matter an industrial worker was not constitutively suspect in the way that a peasant was, always associated with feudalism.

adopted Adam Smith's concept of "previous accumulation"—while renaming it primitive (*ursprüngliche*) accumulation—to refer to the initial acts of violence and dispossession that gave rise to large concentrations of capital.

For Marx, the Enclosure Movement in England was a paradigmatic instance of primitive accumulation. Because he assumed that socialism would follow on the heels of capitalism, he did not envision any need for such accumulation in a socialist regime. Rather, he expected that a solid industrial base would be capitalism's parting gift to communism. However, prerevolutionary Russia—like presocialist China—was a primarily agrarian nation. In recognition of this fact, in the 1920s the Bolshevik economist Evgeny Preobrazhensky theorized primitive *socialist* accumulation as a means of financing a program of industrial development. For him, this was above all an analytic concept. He did not anticipate the use of state violence nor did he support involuntary collectivization, believing that any primitive accumulation in the Soviet Union should take place gradually and be implemented through ordinary bureaucratic means. The notion of primitive socialist accumulation was, and remains, controversial—Preobrazhensky was executed under Stalin—but in the end the USSR reproduced the core feature of the English model: It reorganized its peasantry and transformed the countryside into a source of industrial capital.

A key difficulty with the PRC's use of this strategy was that there was no obvious referent for the term "peasant" in prerevolutionary China. It was a projection of categories of European development, which in turn formed the basis of Marx's stadial account of historical materialism. The word employed by Chinese Communists—*nongmin*—was itself coined by Japanese modernizers in the Meiji era. In order to translate Western concepts, they constructed neologisms using Chinese ideographs while radically resignifying them. Once the word for peasant was exported from Japan back to China, it replaced previously current terms for cultivators (*nongfu*, *nongjia*, *nongren*, and so on), bringing along its modern connotations of rural backwardness.[16]

16 Ibid., 155. Cohen summarizes this process succinctly. It was part of a larger translingual modernization project described by Lydia Liu, *Translingual*

Indeed, classifying the bulk of China's rural population as peasants entails a doctrinaire application of Marxian theory. To fit China into Marx's Eurocentric categories, its countryside was labeled "feudal." Putting aside the question whether the term "feudalism" is adequate even when applied to Europe—the term itself was popularized by Montesquieu in the eighteenth century, long after the demise of its putative referent—China had not known anything akin to feudalism since the Han dynasty (202 BCE–220 CE). Land had been bought and sold for nearly two millennia, and historically fields were cultivated mostly by smallholding tenants. One source of confusion was a form of traditional two-tier ownership of land that had permitted the landlord to retain the rights to the "subsoil" while the tenant owned the "topsoil," or use rights—an arrangement known as "one field, two masters" (*yitian liangzhu*), especially widespread in the fertile Yangtze Delta. By the sixteenth century, this arrangement had evolved into a well-established form of ownership frequently characterized as permanent tenancy.

Marxian historiographers interpreted permanent tenancy as a form of feudal servitude. To be sure, it was structurally similar to certain forms of feudal ownership that distinguished between "direct ownership" (*dominium directum*) by a lord and "ownership of the use" (*dominium utile*) by his vassal, for example. However, a distinction between ownership and use is not specific to feudalism. On the contrary, prior to the

Practice: Literature, National Culture, and Translated Modernity—China, 1900–1937 (Stanford, CA: Stanford University Press, 1995). Given this history, whether we choose to characterize Chinese smallholders at any one time or place as "peasants" or "farmers" is in many respects an ideological choice. One may well question whether it is appropriate to continue to call China's rural citizens today "peasants" rather than "farmers." Nevertheless, the legal and administrative distinction between rural and urban citizens remains in place, even as their social and economic statuses continue to evolve. For the sake of consistency, throughout this book I use the term "peasant" primarily to index a legal and administrative category of persons without assuming that it necessarily corresponds to any specific social identity.

emergence of modern exclusive forms of property, it was the norm rather than the exception.[17]

Moreover, its sinister designation notwithstanding, permanent tenancy did not bind Chinese cultivators either to the land or the landlord in perpetuity or otherwise, nor did the landlord enjoy extra-economic powers over tenants in the manner of his European counterpart. Rather, it permitted tenants to stay on their land indefinitely *if* they so desired, in effect *protecting* them from being dispossessed in the manner of European peasants. In fact, permanent tenants could buy, sell, or mortgage their topsoil interests at will. Put simply, they were legally free tenant farmers in a commercialized agrarian economy. There is no question that they could—and often did—suffer extreme economic hardship, but that hardship arose from their subjection to markets, not from feudal bondage.

Given the extensive commodification of land and the commercialization of agriculture, we might ask why late imperial China had not witnessed a large-scale consolidation of fields akin to the Enclosure Movement in England. To answer the question, we must distinguish analytically two distinct processes that were part of the Enclosure Movement, even as they tended to unfold in tandem in practice. In the first place, the land of the feudal commons became commodified and was divided into alienable pieces of individually owned land. Second, since many of the resulting plots were too small to be viable even for subsistence agriculture, they were ultimately consolidated into larger units appropriate for commercial farming. As a result of these two processes, newly landless commoners were transformed into laborers, first in the service of capitalist agriculture and ultimately in industrial capitalism.

In China the first step—the commodification of land—had already taken place, a millennium and a half earlier than in Europe. Over time, the increasingly alienable nature of land did in fact lead to progressively larger

17 See generally James Q. Whitman, *From Masters of Slaves to Lords of Lands: The Transformation of Ownership in the Western World* (Cambridge: Cambridge University Press, 2025).

holdings, albeit with notable regional variation. In response, many dynasties inaugurated their reigns by breaking up large estates and thus inhibiting the emergence of the kind of vast *latifundia* that came to dominate Imperial Rome, for example. The Tang dynasty, perhaps most notably, promoted the so-called equal-field system (*juntian zhidu*), or the nationalization of agricultural land and its reallocation by the state to taxpaying cultivators, with periodic redistributions to ensure that land allocations remained equitable over time. The utopian scheme never became the norm, however, and by the twelfth century the tenant household established itself as the main production unit, with extensive wage-labor based farms largely disappearing by the end of the seventeenth century.

In addition to dynastic policies favoring tenants over landlords, China's legal system contributed to this outcome. Notably, in contrast to England where the practice of primogeniture helped prevent the fragmentation of manorial estates, in China partible inheritance among male heirs was the norm. At the same time, many features of permanent tenancy protected cultivators from dispossession. Although the landlord's right to subsoil was fully commodified, there was a range of largely customary limitations on the alienation of topsoil rights. For example, tenants could not be evicted simply for failing to pay rent. Even if they fell into arrears or mortgaged their subsoil rights, they could be ousted from their land only when the money they owed was tantamount to the full purchase price of the land. Moreover, even when land was sold voluntarily, in the late imperial period land transfers frequently took the form of a so-called live sale (*huomai*). This entailed a kind of conditional tenancy, with sellers retaining a right to redeem the land they had sold—a right that was frequently exercised. All of this stood in contrast to England, where evolving norms of collateralized lending increasingly allowed mortgage holders to seize debtors' property upon default. In fact, struggling cultivators who had not been dispossessed outright through enclosures more often than not lost their land for indebtedness.[18]

18 These legal differences are described and assessed in greater historical and comparative detail in Taisu Zhang, *The Laws and Economics of Confucianism:*

Why, we may ask, was the Chinese imperial government more inclined to side with tenants while the Parliament in England advanced the interests of the gentry? Indeed, the latter part of the Enclosure Movement consisted primarily of parliamentary enclosures enacted through private bills. From a Marxian viewpoint, this should not surprise us. After the Glorious Revolution, the Parliament was transformed into a landholding oligarchy—functionally the legislative committee of the ruling class, if not quite its executive branch. The Qing rulers, in contrast, prioritized social stability, and unlike the Stuart monarchs they succeeded in preventing the emergence of extensive concentrations of landed wealth, thus reducing the risk of large-scale popular antagonism as well as a potential challenge to their own power. Even in instances where formal law was ambiguous, imperial pro-farmer rhetoric gave tenants ideological cover as they bargained with landowners over the shape of the customary norms that governed their relationship on the ground.[19]

Beyond these political differences, the two countries had very different land-population ratios. By the late imperial era, there was no arable land left to claim even as China's population continued to increase. In a phenomenon that has been called China's "Industrious Revolution," it embarked on a labor-intensive path of development. Its reliance on risiculture is a prime example: Rice is one of the most efficient crops, as it yields the most calories per acre, but it is also one of the most labor-intensive ones. England, on the other hand, had a smaller population relative to its land. Although it too was under demographic stress, its ratio of land to population remained more favorable than China's, and emigration to colonies relieved some of the pressure as well. Hence, development in England took a relatively more capital-intensive route, with rural enclosures generating a surplus for investment, first for agrarian capitalism and ultimately for

---

Kinship and Property in Preindustrial China and England (Cambridge: Cambridge University Press, 2017).

19 Thanks to Taisu Zhang for this formulation.

the labor-saving technologies of the Industrial Revolution. In Jan Luiten van Zanden's succinct formulation, "China didn't 'miss' the Industrial Revolution—it didn't need it." Accordingly, it also did not need to dispossess its peasantry.[20]

Land Reform and Collectivization of Agriculture

In 1949, the PRC was determined to yoke the Industrial Revolution to its communist one, as the Soviet Union had done. To provide the urban socialist worker with the support he needed, China's countryside would need to be converted into a resource for industrial development. The PRC adopted a two-stage approach to remaking its peasants and their relationship to land. The first step was land reform, or the redistribution

---

20 Jan Luiten van Zanden, "Before the Great Divergence: The Modernity of China at the Onset of the Industrial Revolution," *VOXEU*, Jan. 26, 2011, cepr.org. Van Zanden's observation is part of a larger debate about why and when the developmental paths of preindustrial England and China diverged. The debate is too long to summarize here, but it is centered around Kenneth Pomeranz, *The Great Divergence: China, Europe, and the Making of the Modern World Economy* (Princeton, NJ: Princeton University Press, 2000). Pomeranz attributes much of England's rise to what he calls its "windfall" from the New World—essentially a form "primitive accumulation" in Marxian parlance, although Pomeranz does not employ the Marxian term. It should be noted that Pomeranz's analysis is focused almost exclusively on land-based resources, failing to take into account that Europe's "windfall" from America took also the form of surplus labor extracted from slaves who were in turn imported from Africa. On slavery as a form of primitive accumulation in the New World, see Robin Blackburn, *The Making of New World Slavery: From the Baroque to the Modern, 1492–1800* (London: Verso Books, 2010). For a critique of Pomeranz that emphasizes differences in China's and England's internal social and economic organization, especially class and property relations, see Robert Brenner and Christopher Isett, "England's Divergence from China's Yangzi Delta: Property Relations, Microeconomics, and Patterns of Development," *Journal of Asian Studies* 61, no. 2 (2002).

of nearly half of existing farmland, along with associated draft animals and agricultural tools. This served both to break up the power of landlords who had resisted the regime and to reward the peasantry for their loyalty as revolutionary allies. The next step was the collectivization of agricultural production, which would help overcome peasants' "feudal" attachment to their individual plots of land while at the same time enabling the state to extract rural resources more effectively.

China's so-called peasants were not feudal serfs, as we have seen, and by historic standards the properties of many of the landlords targeted by the Land Reform were small-to-medium sized. Nonetheless, there was no question that the overall pattern of distribution of land was highly unequal. Even the Nationalist government had recognized this and sought to address it, like many other dynastic founders had done—albeit with little success. The CCP, however, had a reservoir of experience on which it could draw, as it had already begun redistributing land in bases it had established during the Long March in the areas under its control, collectively known as the Chinese Soviet Republic.

After its official establishment in 1949, the PRC was governed mostly by means of administrative decrees and regulations. Significantly, it approached land redistribution as a *legal* project. In early 1950 it promulgated two major laws, the Land Reform Law and the Marriage Law (apart from organic laws setting up the structures of the state, no other major statutes were passed until the beginning of the reform era in 1978). As we have seen, the Marriage Law sought to transform China's "feudal" social structures. Correspondingly, the Land Reform Law took aim at its "feudal" economic foundation. Compared to the explosive violence that had attended the collectivization of land in the Soviet Union, the Chinese Land Reform was far more orderly; it was peaceful in many regions, while in others peasants took advantage of the opportunity to exact vengeance on their erstwhile landlords, especially in the early phases prior to 1949.

For one thing, the PRC followed a unique schema of land redemption in contrast to the Soviet practice of simple confiscation. In order to know what to distribute, from whom, and to whom, it was necessary to distinguish among the various classes in the countryside. Identifying entirely landless farm laborers was simple. Peasants in turn were divided into rich, middle, and poor ones based on the extent to which they relied on the exploitation of wage labor to help cultivate their fields. The political and administrative methods by which these determinations were made were far from exact and they had been contested ever since they were first employed in the revolutionary bases. As a whole, however, the process was targeted primarily at landlords, in contrast to the Soviet Union's explicit policy of dekulakization, or elimination of not only landlords but prosperous peasants (*kulaks*) as well.

At the end of the process each household received its individual allocation of land. This gave rise to a private agricultural sector in the countryside, apart and distinct from the state-controlled urban economy. From a historical perspective, then, the Land Reform was not so much a revolutionary transformation as a return to a traditional pattern of smallholding. But it was only the beginning. Collecting taxes from over 100 million rural households exceeded the state's administrative capacity. The next step was to collectivize peasants' private holdings and subject them to more direct control. Yet submitting to such a plan was not what newly empowered peasants had in mind. They preferred to cultivate their farms to satisfy their families' needs, not those of the state, and they certainly did not wish to subsidize the privileged existence of industrial workers.

So as not to alienate its rural base, the Party moved slowly at first, encouraging the formation of voluntary low-level peasant cooperatives. In Marx's view, cooperatives were a potentially useful legal form in the transition to socialism. To the extent that they are run by workers themselves, they abolish the opposition between labor and capital, even if the workers become for the time being "their own capitalist," as Marx put it.[21] At the same time, cooperatives served the ideological goal of preventing income polarization among peasants. At the next stage, the PRC began to combine small cooperatives based on contract into larger collectives in which private ownership was abolished entirely: Land, livestock, and agricultural implements all became collective property.

21 Marx, *Capital*, vol. 3, 571.

Importantly, the PRC never nationalized rural land, which remained legally under peasant ownership. This represented an ideological concession to peasants and made China an outlier among socialist states. By comparison, they were never the object of the kind of overt hostility that was directed at their Russian counterparts. The legal scholar Scott Newton characterizes the highly coercive Soviet collectivization as "the conversion of the peasantry into state serfs."[22] But despite the more lenient nature of China's collectivization, it was enacted for the same purpose: primitive socialist accumulation. The state was able to wrest an increasingly large portion of the agricultural surplus, primarily through compulsory "purchases" of all grain above subsistence level at state-mandated prices. The ideological concession of collective ownership notwithstanding—peasants working their own land for themselves—in China, too, the state became in effect the peasants' new landlord. Over time, its grain quotas grew increasingly draconian, reaching ultimately lethal levels during the Great Leap Forward.

To make this regime even more inequitable, not only were the privileges of the urban workforce funded by rural resources, but they were also exclusive to urban citizens. The state never established a system of universal welfare based on national citizenship. Only urban citizens in state-owned enterprises enjoyed full access to state-sponsored privileges. Once the collectivization of agriculture was complete, each rural commune was responsible for the welfare of its members. In circumstances such as crop failure, this could mean even famine unless the central government intervened.[23]

---

22 Scott Newton, *Law and the Making of the Soviet World: The Red Demiurge* (Abingdon: Routledge, 2015), 135.

23 Up to one-third of the grain procured by the state was resold and redistributed in the countryside at subsidized rates to alleviate the risk of hunger. Tim Oakes, "China's Market Reforms: Whose Human Rights Problem?," in Timothy B. Weston and Lionel M. Jensen, eds., *China Beyond the Headlines* (New York: Rowman and Littlefield, 2000), 295–326.

In the end this inequality was justified by the PRC's unique legal distinction between rural and urban land. An agricultural collective not only lived off the land it cultivated but legally it also owned that land. Even though the countryside subsidized the urban economy through coercive extractions, it never became a formal part of the planned economy, which was limited to state-owned entities. Subject to exactions by the state yet officially outside its corporatist framework, peasants remained responsible for themselves, while urban workers were acknowledged to be fully dependent on the state and hence in need of, and eligible for, routine state support.

While land reform had represented a return to the historical norm of smallholding, the collectivization of agriculture *was* truly revolutionary. For a historical precedent, one has to go back to the Zhou dynasty (1046–256 BCE), into the midst of the feudal period before the establishment of a centralized empire—"feudal" not in the ideological socialist sense but in a more historically grounded one. The so-called well-field system, promoted in the late Zhou by the Confucian thinker Mencius—second only to the Master himself—envisioned a regime of communal land ownership, with each field divided into eight square plots among eight households and arranged around a ninth one in the middle. While each household cultivated its own plot, they were collectively responsible for the middle plot for the benefit of the lord. (The system was called "well-field" since the Chinese character for well [井] looks roughly like the nine-fold division of land the system envisions.)

That one has to go back to the Zhou for a precedent is instructive, suggesting that China's collectivization was more akin to a *re*-feudalization of the countryside than its de-feudalization. To the extent that a rural collective was premised on communal cultivation, it was a socialist commons of sorts, with villagers acting in collaboration. Admittedly, this was a feudalism turned upside down. Like their feudal counterparts, socialist villagers, too, were ranked according to status categories, but here former landlords ranked at the bottom and the poorest peasants at the top. What was genuinely feudal was the fact that class labels were assigned to households, not individuals, and they were inherited patrilineally, becoming thus "more like the estates in France's *ancien régime*," in Lucien Bianco's characterization.[24] In effect, categories of structural economic analysis were transformed into quasi-feudal status markers assigned to individual bodies.

Yet from the opposite perspective, collectivization can also be seen as achieving what Chinese landlords, unlike their English counterparts, had not been able to accomplish systematically: consolidating fragmented holdings into larger units, making it possible to cultivate them more efficiently under a single owner—in this case, the Chinese state. Which analogy we prefer depends in part on whom we choose to regard as the "real" owner. If we view the collective as the true owner of its assets—as it was, legally speaking—we do have a socialist commons organized in terms of quasi-feudal hierarchies. On the other hand, if we choose to regard the state as the true owner—juridical niceties notwithstanding—we might liken it to a post-Enclosure capitalist landowner who has successfully consolidated fragmented holdings into large ones, with the important qualification that here the consolidation serves to advance primitive *socialist* accumulation.

However, even if we consider the state the true owner, its ownership retains a feudal guise as well. Like the capitalist English landlord, the state has indeed created a consolidated enclosure, but unlike its capitalist counterpart, it has done so without dispossessing the peasantry. In fact, the state does not pay the peasants for their labor, as a capitalist landlord would do. Instead, the peasants submit to the state whatever they produce beyond and above their own requirements for subsistence. In this respect, the state looks again more like a lord exacting tribute rather than a landlord collecting a fixed rent.

The fact that we can liken the agricultural collective to both the feudal European commons *and* the enclosures that displaced it suggests the partial nature of the analogy, as does the undecidability of who was the "real" owner of the collective. In some ways, it surely *was* akin to a

24 Lucien Bianco, *Stalin and Mao: A Comparison of the Russian and Chinese Revolutions* (Hong Kong: Chinese University of Hong Kong Press, 2018), 59.

socialist commons, based on communal—though not always egalitarian—norms of Chinese village life. Yet to the extent that the state ceaselessly intervened in the collective's autonomy and was able to extract its due at will, its members were more akin to villeins of the state.

War Against Nature

By 1958, rural collectivization had been completed. However, industrial production was not advancing at a rate high enough to satisfy Mao Zedong. The lack of steel in particular had become a bottleneck that was slowing down the growth of heavy industry. To address the shortage, Mao Zedong announced that China would overtake Britain in steel production in fifteen years and catch up with the United States in twenty. This laid the stage for the Great Leap Forward (1958–62), a disastrous campaign that produced sky-high mountains of useless scrap iron and led to one of the largest famines in history. As part of the campaign, the Chairman reorganized the state-owned sector, which was initially based on the highly centralized Soviet model. The control of an increasing number of SOEs was transferred from central ministries to provincial governments in order to make them more responsive to local conditions. But while the urban economy was being decentralized, the agrarian economy was consolidated even further. At the same time, steel production was declared to be everyone's job, with peasants, too, being called to perform industrial labor.

In the countryside, this meant converting collectives into even larger people's communes. Because the vast bulk of industrial capital remained invested in the state sector, increases in rural productivity had to be gained from harnessing peasants' underutilized labor. In order to accomplish this, communes took over the operations of the people's committees on the township level, merging the economic functions of the agricultural collective with the local institutions of the Party-state. Villages below the township level were converted into new subunits known as brigades, further subdivided into teams. These steps represented a revolutionary leap in the reach of government into society. For some two millennia, the county magistrate had been the lowest-ranking imperial official, with a single magistrate overseeing as many as 300,000 people by the late Qing. In the Republican period, the Nationalist government's writ notoriously did not run beyond the cities under its control. Now the arm of the state stretched all the way to the village for the first time, transforming its social and economic foundations.

Although they were generally the object of economic extractions by the state rather than recipients of subsidies, communes were in important ways structurally similar to SOEs. They, too, came to combine many of the functions of the state, the market, and the family. In addition to scaling up agriculture and merging it with local government, the communes—like SOEs—socialized various household tasks. The colloquial phrase "everyone eating from the same pot" (*chi daguo fan*) became a political metaphor for describing a system where everyone shared in labor as well as its fruits. For a brief period, communes literalized the metaphor, constructing large canteens where everyone was allowed to eat at any time, freeing women to take on other tasks—such as building furnaces for smelting iron in their backyards.

In addition to conscripting peasants to take on industrial labor, the Great Leap Forward represented a new stage in their relationship to land. We have seen that Marx regarded man's relationship to nature as oppositional: Labor is a process whereby man "subjects the play of [nature's] forces to his own sovereign power."[25] Although nature is clearly an active force, it can be domesticated through labor. Accordingly, work is the appropriate means to acquire "sovereignty" over it. Mao Zedong, however, was no longer content merely to *work* the land to appropriate nature's bounty. He declared outright *war* on it. In doing so, he extended a military idiom that had come to permeate civilian life—for example, designating agricultural production units as "brigades"—to an entirely new sphere.

Although revolutionizing China's productive capacity was the top priority during the Great Leap Forward, the concern with class struggle

25 Marx, *Capital*, vol. 1, 283.

didn't simply disappear. Rather, enemies of the people took on new forms. In the Great Leap Forward, they came to include animals. The so-called four pests (*si hai*)—much like the counterrevolutionary classes before them—became the object of a major campaign: rats, sparrows, flies, and mosquitoes. Chinese socialist rhetoric—like most, if not all, humanist ideologies—routinely likened its enemies to animals, subhuman and unqualified for inclusion among the people. The analogy was now reversed, turning animals into enemies. Once declared, the war against nature was fought with all weapons available. This included pots and pans, which people were ordered to bang as loudly as possible in order to prevent sparrows from "stealing" the people's grain and to make them eventually fall from the sky in sheer exhaustion.

Tragically, the war against sparrows in particular was far too successful. In Hebei alone, schoolchildren were reported to have killed an improbably precise number of 234,856 sparrows, exemplifying the ultimately disastrous practice of producing misleading and often fictitious reports in order to satisfy administrative mandates from above.[26] The people soon learned that the sparrows were in fact people's allies, not enemies, by virtue of the natural pest control they provided. This shortsightedness led to even greater agricultural losses and contributed to the Great Famine, along with the diversion of agrarian labor into quixotic schemes to fashion steel out of thin air.

The abysmal failure of the Great Leap Forward was followed by a return to smaller collectives and relative normalcy, until the next political convulsion, the onset of the Great Proletarian Cultural Revolution in 1966. As the name of the movement suggests, this was not a war against nature but culture, aimed at the corrupt mindset of revisionist cadres and "capitalist-roaders." Letting go of the dream of a political alchemy that would turn willpower into grain and steel, Mao Zedong now sought a transformation of society itself. This demanded a full-scale return to class struggle, fought by militarized youth fashioned into Red Guards.

26 Stevan Harrell, *An Ecological History of Modern China* (Seattle: University of Washington Press, 2023), 133.

At least for a moment, it reversed the hierarchy between city and country as urban youth in particular were sent to the countryside to learn from their rural counterparts. It also marked a renewed emphasis on prerevolutionary class background and family origin (*chushen*) and a rekindled commitment to global revolution, but one that would no longer be led by the Soviet Union with China as its "younger brother." Having broken permanently with Moscow, Mao Zedong offered himself as the leader of the Third World, united against the imperialism of *both* superpowers, the United States as well as the Soviet Union.

Although the Great Helmsman's efforts fell short of revolutionizing the world, the ideological force of Maoism was contagious. Over the course of the global sixties, it led to the establishment of Maoist factions in socialist movements around the world, including even among the Black Panthers on the faraway shores of North America.[27] This was indeed a global extension of the Cultural Revolution, a deployment of culture as a diplomatic and political weapon, meant to contrast with the United States' and the Soviet Union's ultimate reliance on military force. Mao Zedong dismissed the two superpowers' atomic weapons as a "paper tiger" that could not stand up to the global insurgency led by China, with the Third World constituting the world's "countryside" that would encircle the "cities" of the First World.

Feudalism Redux

In this chapter, we have seen how the making of the Chinese working class was at the same time the making of the Chinese peasantry. They were both fashioned by the state, which segregated them spatially: Peasants were tied to their rural collectives while workers in the technical sense were attached to their urban work units. The latter were the converse of the former and could not have existed without it, and it was these two classes' differentiated relationship to land and labor that allowed the state to direct a continuous

27 See Robin D. G. Kelley and Betsy Esch, "Black Like Mao: Red China and Black Revolution," *Souls* 1, no. 4 (1999): 6–41.

flow of rural resources to cities. To be sure, over time this flow tended to diminish: As industrial production grew and agriculture became a smaller component of the China's GDP, relatively more resources were devoted to agriculture.[28] However, the bulk of capital continued to be invested in heavy industry rather than the mechanization of agriculture. While agricultural yields continued to grow, much of that growth resulted from increases in the expenditure of labor rather than capital, such as labor-intensive collective irrigation projects.

Given this overall structural imbalance, what kept the disadvantaged peasants in their place, literally? As we have seen, the chief mechanism for restricting internal mobility was the so-called *hukou* ("household") registration system. This practice had millennial roots as the basis of agricultural taxation, which had been the chief source of imperial revenue. The PRC, however, put the system to radically new uses, tying a number of vital benefits to a person's residence, ranging from housing to schooling to medical care to food rations. As noted in the introduction, to be categorized a "peasant" (*nongmin*), as opposed to a city-dwelling "worker" (*gongren*), was thus not only an ideological label or a social identity but a legally enforced administrative status as well.

Moreover, once established, one's residence was virtually untransferable, passing down to one's offspring matrilineally. It became a sorting mechanism that divided the entire population into essentially two groups: a privileged set of urban residents and a subordinated rural one. Which of the two Chinas one was born into had a decisive significance for the trajectory of a person's life, to the point that the agricultural economist Wen Tiejun characterizes the rural-urban distinction as "the fundamental institution of China."[29] Although land reform had initially established

---

28 Ching Pao-yu, "How Sustainable is China's Agriculture? A Closer Look at China's Agriculture and Chinese Peasants," in *Revolution and Counterrevolution: China's Continuing Class Struggle Since Liberation* (Paris: Foreign Languages Press, 2021), 263. I thank Yan Hairong for bringing this source to my attention.

29 Wen Tiejun, *Ten Crises: The Political Economy of China's Development 1949–2020* (Singapore: Palgrave Macmillan, 2021), 200.

a range of fine-grained class distinctions, they were eventually overwhelmed by a binary system of residential segregation. Over time, even landlords and "rich peasants" became assimilated into the generic category of peasants, as the term came to refer simply to China's rural population. Over time the registration system transformed rural poverty into an inherited condition.

Despite the fact that peasants became de facto second-class citizens in the revolutionary republic for which they had fought, it is vital to emphasize that their condition was one of relative—although significant—inequality. Even as the state continued to transfer resources from the country to the city, material austerity was accompanied by major improvements in the quality of rural life. The state made crucial investments in its human capital in two areas in particular: health care and education. Mass vaccinations helped eliminate most contagious disease while "barefoot doctors" waged a battle against infant mortality. In the span between 1949 and 1978, life expectancy doubled, while elementary education became increasingly accessible, especially for girls.

At the same time, it is important to recognize that the hierarchical city-country divide that came to dominate Chinese socialism—ultimately based on the legal differentiation between urban and rural land—is not simply a traditional prejudice that somehow persisted into socialism. On the contrary, in the Confucian state ideology that preceded it, farmers were glorified, ranking above merchants and other urbanites who did not engage in tilling the land, the primary productive activity. Moreover, even though late imperial China was far more urbanized than Europe, city-dwellers enjoyed no special legal privileges, in contrast to Europe, where "free cities" were exempt from feudal exactions, famously promising *Stadtluft macht frei*. Indeed, it was precisely this freedom that allowed cities in Europe to emerge as centers of nonagricultural production that gave birth to a new and unruly class of bourgeois subjects without personal loyalties or territorial attachments.

In contrast, many cities in late imperial China were more akin to the classical cities of Rome: administrative units that functioned as elite hubs of culture and consumption, defined neither by corporate charters nor by associated liberties, and which relied on their hinterland for necessities and on long-range trade for luxuries. Indeed, the bulk of local trade was unidirectional, flowing from the countryside to cities. Even major cities that were primarily economic rather than administrative centers were not sharply distinguished from the countryside. Many urban residents, including wealthy merchants and guild members, viewed themselves as merely temporary sojourners in the city, returning regularly to their native places which continued to define their social identity. Nor did the imperial bureaucracy differentiate between city and country administratively, treating them as part of a single unified polity.

In short, the categorical rural-urban legal distinction is a Chinese *socialist* contribution. It provided the crucial foundation for the making of an urban working class, which was at the same time the making of a rural peasantry. In socialist theory, the revolution freed the Chinese peasant from his bondage and gave him land, first as private property and then under collective ownership. Paradoxically, tenant farmers who had certainly often been poor but not tied to soil legally, became for the first time permanently attached to the land they tilled. As we have noted, their ostensible liberation effectively re-feudalized, rather than de-feudalized, them. What is more, not only were they made legal owners of land they were unable to leave, but *because* of their land ownership they were deemed self-sufficient and ineligible for privileges the state accorded to its urban workers who remained under the state's direct care (and control).

The comparison to Europe again underscores the paradox. To borrow the historian Eugen Weber's famous phrase, the French Revolution turned the nation's "peasants into Frenchmen"—rather than dispossessing the peasantry, it transformed them into citizen-farmers who owned the fields they cultivated.[30] To be sure, the new regime of private property came with no guarantee of permanent ownership. Marx observed sharply that as many of the new freeholders fell into debt, "the feudal obligation that went with the land was replaced by the mortgage," thus

30 Eugen Weber, *Peasants into Frenchmen: The Modernization of Rural France, 1870–1914* (Stanford, CA: Stanford University Press, 1976).

subjecting the French farmer, like his English counterpart, to the ultimate expropriation of his land.[31] China's socialist revolution, in contrast to the French bourgeois one, performed the reverse procedure, transforming a nation of farmers into peasants. It would be an exaggeration to claim that the PRC reduced its rural citizens to quasi-serfdom in the manner of the Soviet state farms—the notorious *sovhozy*—but in the process "worker" and "peasant" turned into inherited administrative statuses that indexed a quasi-feudal peasanthood on the one hand and a socialist labor aristocracy on the other. The former was defined by its ownership of land, the latter by the labor it provided to the state.

31 Marx, *The Eighteenth Brumaire of Louis Bonaparte*, 126–7.

2

Remaking the Peasant: Rural Industrialization, 1978–1994

Agricultural surplus product is the basis of all surplus product and thereby of all civilisation.

—Ernest Mandel, *Marxist Economic Theory*

The dominant narrative ascribes China's economic success from the very beginning of the reform era to the rise of private entrepreneurship and a corresponding retreat by the state from the economy. That story is essentially a lazy projection of the tenets of free-market ideology onto China's experience. It not only misdescribes that experience, but it also limits our ability to understand the subsequent development of Chinese state capitalism and its global significance. This chapter revisits this story and details the profound consequences the early reforms had for rural China and its relationship to land, labor, and the state. As we will see in subsequent chapters, much of Chinese capitalism's global success has been subsidized by enduring socialist legacies dating to the early reform era.

Conventionally, the beginning of China's reform era is dated to the Party's issuance of a major communiqué at the Third Plenary Session of its Eleventh Central Committee on December 22, 1978. Seeking to put the Cultural Revolution behind, the Party announced that class struggle had been in the main won. This provided an ideological justification for a renewed focus on developing the forces of production, signaling a shift from continuous revolution to a primary concern with economic development. Despite its having come to signify retroactively the beginning of the reform era that ensued, the communiqué could not have been further from a blueprint for a structural transformation of the Chinese economy as a whole, and it certainly did not outline a platform for today's state capitalism. Committing itself to the enactment of so-called Four Modernizations—the strengthening of agriculture, industry, defense, and science/technology—the Party's paramount concern was rural poverty, which it had neglected far too long.

The principal reform was a relatively modest reorganization of farmland. The communiqué simply declared that "small plots of land for private use by commune members, their domestic side-occupations, and village fairs are necessary adjuncts of the socialist economy."[1] This idea was far from unprecedented. After the Great Famine had put a tragic end to the Great Leap Forward, similar steps had been undertaken in several parts of the country, but those measures had been eventually shut down by Mao as ideologically objectionable, only to reemerge in the provinces of Anhui and Sichuan in the early 1970s. At the same time, Mao must be credited, at least in part, with elevating rural poverty itself to a source of official concern. After the initial post-1949 privileging of workers over peasants, the Cultural Revolution had rehabilitated the peasantry politically, elevating it to new ideological heights, and as we saw in chapter 1, masses of students and intellectuals had been sent to the countryside to learn from peasants. When the Cultural Revolution ended, the returnees were intimately familiar with rural poverty and recognized its extent and significance from personal experience.

The reorganization of collectively farmed land was a highly successful one. One of its entirely unintended side effects was the rise of rural industry. Not only did rural industrialization drive the first phase of China's unprecedented economic growth but it also challenged the basic division of labor between city and country, one agricultural and the other industrial. In significant ways, China's early reforms seem to

1 Communiqué of the Third Plenary Session of the Eleventh Central Committee of the Communist Party of China," translated in *Peking Review*, December 29, 1978, 12.

conform to the English experience: In England, too, the dismantling of an agrarian commons gave rise to rural industry. Importantly, though, the new industrial enterprises in England were organized by *private* capital. In contrast to England, the bulk of China's new rural industry was organized in the form of rural collectives known as Township and Village Enterprises (*xiangzhen qiye*). The TVEs' incredible productivity thus presents something of a puzzle. If the success of agriculture resulted from its *decollectivization*, why were new rural industries organized in the form of *collectives*?

Decollectivization of Agriculture

The main item of the economic reforms was an exceedingly simple one, known as the Household Responsibility System (*jiating lianchan chengbao zhi*). Under this system rural collectives were officially permitted to divide up their agricultural land into small plots that were allocated to member households. So long as each household remanded an agreed-upon quota to the collective—that is, fulfilled its household responsibility—it was free to sell the remainder at market price. Today many commentators characterize the Household Responsibility System as a "privatization," or a close approximation of it. It was not. To accept this characterization is to fall into the ideological trap of assuming that the subsequent commodification of rural land—the subject matter of chapter 4—was inevitable and somehow incipient in the first reforms.

Significantly, only the *use* of land was allocated to individual households. That use was not alienable: It could not be transferred to other households or entities. Since land remained collectively owned, it could not be leased, sold, gifted, or passed on to heirs. Put differently, allocated land had use value but no exchange value, as there was no market for its circulation. Moreover, each household's allocation was temporary, subject to periodic reallocation by the collective to ensure that the distribution of land use reflected demographic changes among households and remained equitable over time—an egalitarianism fundamentally opposed to the norms of private property. Finally, a portion of agricultural production still went to the collective and to the urban sector, at state-mandated prices, although the rest could now be sold on the market.

Even as the state continued to extract a surplus from the country, the new system of dual pricing—selling a predetermined grain quota to the state at a state-controlled price and the remainder at market price—altered the peasants' relationship to the state. The state was now less like a feudal lord commanding the peasants' labor and the surplus they produced beyond their subsistence needs. Instead, it became more akin to a commercial landlord who collects a fixed rent, leaving the rest to the cultivator to consume or to sell. In this respect, the arrangement was similar to the presocialist tradition of smallholding.

The Household Responsibility System also led to a greater integration of the countryside. The Maoist commune was built on the utopian ideal of complete, or nearly complete, self-sufficiency of each unit, analogous to the autarky the Great Helmsman sought for China as a nation. Historically, however, the Chinese countryside had been organized around a hierarchy of market towns that connected villages and smaller towns into local and regional networks. The socialist ideal of an archipelago of self-contained units represented a radical departure from this pattern. The emergence of commodity markets revived some of the traditional networks and helped break down the atomized nature of the countryside.

Collectivization of Rural Industry

While the Household Responsibility System was designed to increase the nation's agricultural yield, the speed and extent of its success exceeded official expectations. This success was not an unequivocal blessing, however. The *hukou* registration system and the attendant institutions for controlling peasant mobility were still in place. Over time, they had led to a large, and growing, population surplus in the countryside. More efficient cultivation only exacerbated the problem, with no outlet for the unemployed and underemployed.

But the success of decollectivization had positive unintended consequences as well—most notably, the rapid rise of rural industry, which in turn destabilized the established distinction between city and country. An increasing agricultural surplus became a source of capital which could be invested in industry and that industry in turn could absorb the surplus labor that was no longer needed in agriculture. This is in fact what happened, although no one had planned it. "What took us by surprise completely was the development of township and village industries," Deng Xiaoping subsequently admitted, adding, "This was not something I had thought about."[2]

It was this essentially autochthonous rural industry that drove China's phenomenal economic growth through the mid- to late 1990s. While heavy industry remained the domain of SOEs, the countryside developed various kinds of light industry the state had neglected: machinery, electronics, building materials, chemicals, plastic products, apparel, shoes, and so on. Between 1978 and 1995, TVEs' total output increased at an average rate of 21 percent per year. From 1980 to 1996 their total number leapt from 1.4 million to 23.4 million, and the number of people they employed grew from 30 million to 135 million.[3]

Here we find ourselves at the core of what seems to be a major contradiction in China's development: While the decollectivization of farming led to a (relative) breakup of the socialist agricultural commons, it gave rise to a new kind of *industrial commons*. If it was the decollectivization of agriculture that is supposed to have revitalized it, why did the emerging rural industry organize itself in the form of collectives—the very feature that agriculture seemed to be leaving behind? Despite the key role they played during a period in which China's economy grew at a world-historic pace, it turns out that TVEs are not widely known by nonexperts, nor are they necessarily well understood even by experts.

---

2 Lynn White, *Unstately Power, vol. 1: Local Causes of China's Economic Reforms* (Armonk, NY: M. E. Sharpe, 1998), 96, quoting Deng Xiaoping.

3 See Enrico C. Perotti, Laixiang Sun, and Liang Zou, "State-Owned Versus Township and Village Enterprises in China," *Comparative Economic Studies* 41, nos. 2–3 (1999): 152.

For mainstream observers the superiority of private enterprise is axiomatic. Accordingly, they insist that TVEs *were* private enterprises simply because they *must* have been. To be sure, many were. In an era when collective ownership was the only legal form of enterprise recognized in the countryside, private entrepreneurs had overwhelming ideological and material incentives to cloak themselves in public nomenclature. This was exemplified by so-called red hat (*hong maozi*) entities, or "fake collectives" run by entrepreneurs who paid a fee to the local government for the privilege of operating a privately owned but officially recognized enterprise. Regionally, observers often distinguish between the so-called Sunan and Wenzhou models (also known as the Jiangsu model and Zhejiang model, respectively, on the basis of their provincial locations), the former representing "genuine" collectives and the latter private enterprises in the guise of collective ones.[4] However, there is little question that most TVEs were in fact collectively owned local enterprises. Moreover, it was the TVEs

---

4 TVEs varied regionally also with respect to their sources of capital. Many villages in the southeastern coastal regions reactivated their links to diasporic communities outside of China. Numerous expatriated mainlanders returned from Taiwan and Hong Kong, most notably, bringing capital as well as technical know-how. At the same time, many of the smaller Wenzhou enterprises typically characterized as "private" may be better described as "household enterprises"—a noncapitalist mode of production that can, under certain conditions, compete with private enterprise because it relies primarily on household labor rather than commodified labor. For a theorization of the use of domestic labor as a distinct noncapitalist form of "self-exploitation," see A. V. Chayanov, *The Theory of Peasant Economy* (Madison: University of Wisconsin Press, 1986 [1925]).

In any event, since TVEs were a form of *local* enterprise, their organizational and operational characteristics varied from one local government to the next, and even more across regions. At different times and in different places, they combined public and private elements in distinctive ways and in varying degrees. However, as Jean Oi observes, it is clear that "collectively owned enterprises dominated in most townships and villages in the 1980s." Jean Oi, *Rural China Takes Off: Institutional Foundations of Economic Reform* (Los Angeles: University of California Press, 1999), 58.

under the actual control of rural governments that were responsible for the bulk of the growth generated by rural industry. In short, it was these bona fide public enterprises that were both the vanguard and the mainstay of China's economic revolution in the countryside.[5]

Why, then, did the local state come to provide the chief institutional foundation for emerging rural industry? The reasons are at once historical, political, and fiscal. Historically, rural China has always had abundant labor, and by definition each collective also owned its land. With rising agricultural production, collectives were increasingly able to accumulate capital as well. Yet there was one ingredient that was seemingly missing, and it was perhaps the most crucial of all: an institutional framework for *organizing* the factors of production. More complex than agriculture, industrial enterprise requires structures of authority that exceed the household. In the late 1970s and early 1980s, the local state was the main, if not sole, integrative hierarchy that was left standing in the aftermath of the Cultural Revolution. Therefore, it is hardly surprising that it was the local state that came to provide the template for rural industry.

The experience of the Great Leap Forward is instructive. As we have seen, it sought to address the crisis of rural poverty not only by transforming agriculture but also by introducing industrial production to the countryside. In the end, revolutionary passion alone could not make up for lack of adequate capital and industrial organization, and peasants soon learned that smelting iron in a backyard furnace was not a recipe for high-quality steel. Yet the legacy of the Great Leap Forward was not

5 Supporting this conclusion, Chun Chang and Yijian Wang, among others, note that smaller enterprises were more likely to be privately owned than highly capitalized ones. Chun Chang and Yijian Wang, "The Nature of the Township-Village Enterprise," *Journal of Comparative Economics* 19, no. 3 (1994): 434, 448. Jean Oi similarly observes that collectively organized TVEs were predominant over private ones, with the latter concentrated in "small scale service trades, handicrafts, and small manufacturing"—indeed, likely many of them household enterprises of the kind analyzed by Chayanov, above. See Oi, *Rural China Takes Off*, 62, 67.

purely negative. Even though rural industry had been undercapitalized, peasants had been trained in new skills and the institutional memory of local public enterprise persisted into the reform era, as did many enterprises themselves. Moreover, in the early 1970s, even prior to the official beginning of the reform era in 1978, there had been another wave of state support for the establishment of rural industry, albeit mostly for the traditional purpose of supporting agriculture. There were an estimated 1.5 million such enterprises in 1978.[6] This was not an insignificant number, although they would be vastly outnumbered by the TVEs that emerged in the 1980s and 1990s.

There was a final important development that midwifed the birth of TVEs, namely the fiscal restructuring of the state. Constitutionally the People's Republic of China has been a unitary state since its founding. For administrative purposes it is a pyramid-shaped entity subdivided into five levels of government, with each level reporting to the level immediately above and ultimately to the central government. Prior to the fiscal reform, each level submitted the revenues it collected to the central state, which in turn redistributed them downward according to a central plan. In 1980, this centralized structure was replaced with a new tax responsibility system. The reform's goal was to relieve the central state of its financial liability for provincial and other lower-level governments whose expenses continually exceeded their receipts. Under the new system, the central government permitted each level of government to keep any revenue it collected in excess of a quota, which it negotiated with the level of government immediately above. This reorganization, sometimes described as "fiscal federalism," provided the center with a guaranteed stream of income and sought to make lower levels of government self-financing.

Although revenue quotas were a matter of intense negotiation and not always met, the reform gave local governments for the first time a distinct fiscal identity, subjecting them at least in theory to hard budget constraints. Although the point was to redistribute economic burdens,

6 Stevan Harrell, *An Ecological History of Modern China* (Seattle: University of Washington Press, 2023), 304.

as a corollary, local governments were also allowed to keep any "extrabudgetary" revenue they generated. The tax responsibility system was in effect a fiscal analogue of the agricultural Household Responsibility System, with the central government farming out its tax collection to local governments, much as rural collectives farmed out agricultural production to individual households. Accordingly, the new arrangement came to be referred to as "eating in separate kitchens" (*fenzao chifan*), in contrast to the Maoist ideal of everyone "eating from one big pot" (*chi daguo fan*). Just as households had a strong incentive to invest in their plots, local governments now found themselves with an incentive to invest in commercial undertakings that would generate revenue they could keep. Collectively these enterprises came to be known as TVEs.

The Birth of an Industrial Commons

That there were few alternatives to the collective as a structure of economic organization in the countryside is intuitively appealing, and it is also evident that the fiscal restructuring was a necessary precondition for TVEs' emergence. But even if the collective was the *only* organizational template available, that is not enough to explain *why* it worked in such a spectacular manner—or indeed why it worked at all. Answering that question takes us to a larger debate about the productivity of collectively owned resources. In an oft-cited essay on "The Tragedy of the Commons," published in 1968, the economist *cum* ecologist Garrett Hardin argued that when resources are owned by all, they are effectively owned by no one: No one has an incentive to develop them if the gains are shared by all, resulting in underuse and waste. Alternatively, if it is possible for an individual to appropriate more than his or her fair share, such resources are likely to be looted and overused. What, then, were the local institutions that made the new industrial commons work and prevented it from being plundered by a handful of cadres?

Political scientists offer an essentially political answer, rooted in the specific ways in which rural industry's operation was articulated with the multiple institutions of the local state. Jean Oi characterizes the phenomenon as "local state corporatism," suggesting that in the Chinese countryside the local government functioned in the manner of a business corporation, with local officials acting as a board of directors overseeing the economic affairs of the village.[7] Typically, officials hired private managers to operate TVEs on behalf of the community as a whole, but rather than simply renting out its name to a private entrepreneur for a fee, the local government retained control over strategic decisions as well as profits generated by the enterprise. At the same time, although an individual villager did not have a direct, formal ownership right in them, collectively villagers were the ultimate owners of the community's enterprises, not unlike shareholders of a corporation.

Even though Western social scientists have generally ignored TVEs, economics is the other major field—in addition to political science—which has taken note of them. To be sure, most economists have never even heard of TVEs, but, paradoxically, they have been the object of considerable fascination among a small handful of leading thinkers in the field. This is not necessarily because of their practical import—even though it is extraordinary—but because of the radical challenge they pose to economic theory: Theoretically, they should not exist. As the parable of the tragedy of the commons suggests, no investor—public or private—should be willing to invest in a firm unless the invested assets are legally protected. This has led even prominent economists to dismiss TVEs as perverse hybrids of public and private elements. Most notably, Douglass North—a Nobel laureate who early

7 See Oi, *Rural China Takes Off*. See also Andrew G. Walder, "The County Government as an Industrial Corporation," in Andrew G. Walder, ed., *Zouping in Transition: The Process of Reform in Rural China* (Cambridge, MA: Harvard University Press, 1998), and Che Jiahua and Yingyi Qian, "Institutional Environment, Community Government, and Corporate Governance: Understanding China's Township-Village Enterprises," *Journal of Law, Economics, and Organization* 14, no. 1 (1998): 1–23.

on took an interest in TVEs—complained that "China still does not have well-specified property rights, [TVEs] hardly resemble the standard firm of economics, and [the country] remains to this day a communist dictatorship."[8]

Joseph Stiglitz—also a Nobel Prize winner as well as a former chief economist at the World Bank—takes a more positive view. Declaring TVEs a "brilliantly successful institutional innovation," he argues that they succeeded even in the absence of formal legal entitlements because village officials protected parties' legitimate expectations.[9] Rather than muddled hybrids of the state and the market, TVEs worked precisely *because* they combined aspects of both: They were in effect a creative institutional adaptation to the lack of formally defined property rights at an early stage of legal and economic reform. This is essentially the same explanation as that advanced by political scientists, albeit in a more generic formulation: TVEs were overseen by officials who protected the collective's assets.

These overlapping political and economic analyses are insightful yet inadequate. Observing that the state protected villagers' interests does not explain *how* it was able to do so. For Stiglitz, the state is ultimately a black box—an entity with discrete goals that somehow regulates itself and is able to act in the collective interest of its members. The property scholar Frank Upham offers a more nuanced understanding of the sociology of Chinese rural society. He attributes TVEs' success to a range of inherited informal institutions protecting investors' expectations, concluding that villagers' ownership in TVEs "may actually have been better protected through social and political means than are the much

8 Douglass North, "The Chinese Menu (for Development)," *Wall Street Journal*, April 7, 2005, wsj.com.

9 Stiglitz makes this observation, with two coauthors, in Athar Hussain, Nicholas Stern, and Joseph Stiglitz, "Chinese Reform from a Comparative Perspective," in Peter J. Hammon and Gareth D. Myles, eds., *Incentives, Organization, and Public Economics* (Oxford: Oxford University Press, 2000), 271.

more clearly articulated ownership rights of shareholders in American corporations."[10]

Yet property rights alone—or even their functional equivalent—do not a firm make. An enterprise that is overseen by managers who are distinct from its owners needs also a body of organizational law. Even if local officials were in a position to ensure that TVE managers did not loot the enterprises they ran, what restrained those officials from doing so on their *own* behalf? In the classical formulation of the question, *quis custodiet ipsos custodes*—who will guard the guardians? To answer this question, we must view the Chinese *village as a whole* as a public enterprise of sorts. In effect, it was the law of village government that ordered both the local state *and* local enterprise. Put differently, it also performed the functions of both administrative law and corporation law. Much of this law consisted of uncodified social expectations and local institutions—what we might call the customary law of townships and villages—and it was this law that prevented the plundering of publicly owned resources.

This outline of the organization of rural industry as a kind of industrial commons not only helps explain how it avoided the tragedy predicted by Hardin and economic theorists, but it also suggests the limitations of Hardin's famous analysis even on its own terms. It is striking that he uses the feudal commons as his key historical example of the would-be tragedy of the commons. Indeed, the legions of historians and economists who regard the Enclosure Movement as a necessary step in putting England's feudal lands to more productive use—a view popularized by Adam Smith in *The Wealth of Nations*—seem to confirm Hardin's hard-nosed analysis.

Perhaps the most fundamental limitation of this view is that it projects retrospectively a capitalist rationality onto a noncapitalist social and economic order. In a feudal economy organized around the logic of the commons, there is little profit to be gained by hoarding more than one needs.

10 Frank Upham, "What Are Property Rights Good For? Surprising Lessons from the Chinese Experience," in Guanghua Yu, ed., *Rethinking Law and Development: The Chinese* Experience (New York: Routledge, 2013), 87.

Moreover, the legal scholar Carol Rose reminds us that while the commons may have had multiple owners, that did not mean that it was simply unregulated. On the contrary, it was subject to the common law as well as rules of customary law which governed its use and helped ensure at least a minimum level of participation for everyone in its benefits, including the landless—an outcome Rose calls "the comedy of the commons," or as E. P. Thompson puts it succinctly, "[the commoners] were not without commonsense."[11] Just as England's feudal commons had its own customary law, so did the socialist commons that supported China's rural industry.

It is notable that this socialist commons is also structurally analogous to a set of late imperial institutions I have analyzed elsewhere as "clan corporations." In a political economy organized in Confucian terms, economic enterprise was frequently set up in the form of Confucian lineage organizations. Significantly, in many of these entities, kinship was only a legal fiction, much as corporate personhood is a fiction in the Euro-American tradition of corporation law. This conceptualization gave them a legally recognized status and a potentially multigenerational lifespan that allowed them to pool and manage productive resources over time. Insofar as the enterprises were run by full-time managers, they also entailed a functional separation between ownership and management, similar to the one we have seen in TVEs. Here, though, the gap was closed by the principles of Confucian family law. As kinship entities, they were governed by the norms of local kinship institutions, leaving it ultimately to family law, broadly construed, to perform the functions of modern corporation law. Similarly, it was the local law of village governance, broadly construed, that protected the interests of the community as a whole and helped China's phenomenal economic resurgence from the 1980s through the mid-1990s while providing for a relatively egalitarian allocation of its gains among rural citizens.

---

11 Carol Rose, "The Comedy of the Commons: Custom, Commerce, and Inherently Public Property," *University of Chicago Law Review* 53, no. 3 (1986): 711–81; E. P. Thompson, *Customs in Common: Studies in Traditional Popular Culture* (London: Penguin Books, 1993), 107.

Governing the Industrial Commons

Because TVEs are poorly understood and all too often assumed to be merely socialist fronts for private capital, it is important to examine in some detail the institutions that made them work. By its very constitution, a TVE was a hybrid: part corporation, part commons. Janus-like, it faced both inward and outward. We have already seen that internally it was structured like an industrial corporation with two layers of hierarchy: managers overseeing workers who provided labor in return for wages, and village officials exercising oversight over the managers much like a corporate board. Externally, TVEs were characterized by a division of labor between their passive owners—the villagers—and the officials responsible for monitoring the managers.

But even if we view village officials as a kind of board of directors, how realistic is it to regard the villagers as owners? On the one hand, it is true that TVEs had no identifiable discrete owners. On the other hand, there is no question that as a member of the community each villager had an economic stake in village assets. Even under Maoism there were established norms and institutionalized practices of ownership. According to inherited socialist principles, assets in public enterprises were owned by the citizens of whichever level of government originally funded them: "Whoever invests is the owner and receives the benefits" (*shei touzi, shei suoyou, shei deyi*).[12] Under this theory, the property of an enterprise established by a village belonged to the members of the village as whole, while the right to control the property was exercised by village government, resulting effectively in a division between ownership by the village members and management by the village government.

12 Susan H. Whiting, "The Regional Evolution of Ownership Forms: Shareholding Cooperatives and Rural Industry in Shanghai and Wenzhou," in Jean C. Oi and Andrew G. Walder, eds., *Property Rights and Economic Reform in China* (Stanford, CA: Stanford University Press, 1999), 187.

To be sure, villagers' equity was not transferable. Under the household registration system, they could not even vote with their feet. But while ownership is presumptively transferable in a *private* enterprise, here its absence signifies the fact that TVEs were a form of *public* enterprise, embedded in a larger socialist commons. Hence TVEs also could not simply distribute their profits to individual villagers. Instead, the bulk of them were reinvested in the enterprise while the rest were spent on the provision of public goods, taking the form of quasi-dividends, such as community centers, educational subsidies, and even free water and electricity, in the case of the most prosperous villages—a practice Oi characterizes as "redistributive corporatism."[13] Reflecting this principle, because of their relatively higher pay, TVE managers also typically sought to ensure that at least one member in each local household was employed in a TVE. Correspondingly, insofar as a TVE also employed workers from outside the village, those workers were ordinarily paid less than the villagers.

But this still leaves us with the question: How did this commons hold the village officers accountable to the villagers as a group? Village elections are the most obvious, albeit not necessarily the most effective, institution of village governance. Beginning in 1987, the Organic Law of Village Committees has provided for the election of a three- to seven-member village committee (*cunmin weiyuanhui*). The larger democratic significance of village elections is a matter of debate, but as far as TVEs are concerned, they were not established with an abstract political ideal in mind. The political scientists Kevin O'Brien and Lianjiang Li observe that "they have less to do with liberal ideology or any newfound affection for pluralism and more to do with preventing local officials from thwarting measures designed to reign [*sic*] them in."[14] To the extent that the central government had lost its ability to exert effective control in villages—because of the autonomy they had won during the Cultural

13 Oi, *Rural China Takes Off*, 79–80.

14 Kevin J. O'Brien and Lianjiang Li, *Rightful Resistance in Rural China* (Cambridge: Cambridge University Press, 2006), 65.

Revolution—it now sought to recruit villagers themselves as watchdogs.

Village elections may not have lived up to the democratic expectations that many had of them, but at least in some instances villagers have in fact used them to police TVEs by overturning manipulated elections, reclaiming diverted village funds, and auditing suspicious government accounts. And although the mere existence of formally articulated legal rights does not guarantee that they will be enforced, a growing awareness of such rights has motivated villagers to realize them also through informal means when the state has failed to uphold them. Staging a collective protest can become a kind of "class action," and an expanding rights consciousness in Chinese villages has given rise to the use of traditional protest tactics in combination with assertions of formal rights, resulting in an admixture of Maoist rhetoric and claims based on local citizenship.

Starting in the 1980s, many villages began enacting so-called village compacts (*cungui minyue*), drawing on a Confucian tradition dating from the Ming dynasty (1368–1644 CE). This practice is codified in the Organic Law of Village Committees, which calls for village assemblies to issue charters with management regulations. Insofar as such charters go beyond general ethical exhortations and provide rules for village governance, they can play a role at least roughly analogous to corporation bylaws. As this selective reliance on Confucian institutional precedents suggests, TVEs combined not only the economic logic of markets with the political logic of the local state; they also drew on the reemergence of an earlier, never wholly expurgated idiom of kinship-based trust, defined not only by blood ties but by metaphoric extensions of kinship as well.

Despite the Party's efforts to abolish Confucianism as a feudal superstition, communities' collective interest in their TVEs was articulated consistently in both political and kinship terms. For example, the relationship between a local government and a TVE was described typically as a "father-son" relationship. Similarly, when TVE managers were caught in relatively minor acts of misbehavior, officials sought to address them locally, "within the family," whenever possible.[15]

In short, TVEs were also embedded in, and structured by, an older *kinship commons*. The invocation of family was not merely metaphorical as economic reforms gave older kinship structures a new material basis. In some locales, especially in coastal Southeast China, the strongest non-market institution in the beginning of the reform era was not necessarily the state but presocialist lineage organizations. Maoism had rendered them formally invisible, yet what took place after 1949 was frequently a mere relabeling of kinship-based entities as local state structures.

When agriculture was collectivized in the 1950s, what became socialist communes and brigades were often preexisting towns and villages. In many areas, especially along the southeast coast, prerevolutionary villages were controlled by a single lineage—instances of former clan corporations organized in terms of Confucian kinship norms. When markets were first established in the beginning of the reform era, it is no surprise that in many villages presocialist kinship norms continued to structure local politics as well as the local economy, with real and fictive lineage ties providing a social foundation for the pooling of productive resources. In her study of informal institutions of accountability in rural China, the political scientist Lily Tsai finds that the existence of local lineage organizations correlates highly with the provision of public goods which, as we have seen, was one of the principal means by which TVEs distributed their profits to the community.[16]

In sum, in many places, norms of Confucian family law that had governed enterprises in the late imperial era reemerged and recombined

15 Lina Song, "Convergence: A Comparison of Township Firms and Local State Enterprises," in William A. Byrd and Qingsong Lin, eds., *China's Rural Industry: Structure, Development, and Reform* (Oxford: Oxford University Press, 1990), 396; Oi, *Rural China Takes Off*, 157.

16 Lily L. Tsai, *Accountability Without Democracy: Solidary Groups and Public Goods Provision in Rural China* (Cambridge: Cambridge University Press, 2007), 48–186.

with the rural institutions of the socialist state to produce a novel, hybrid law of village governance, broadly construed, which in turn supported a new kind of industrial commons.

Twilight of Collective Industry

Whatever TVEs' virtues may have been, we need not idealize them any more than we ought to idealize the feudal commons that gave way to capitalism in Europe. It is enough to recognize that while TVEs may defy orthodox theories of the organization of enterprise and of economic development, many of them were evidently remarkably successful over a significant period of time, helping lift millions of rural Chinese out of poverty and driving the nation's economic growth during the first phase of the reforms. As we have seen, a typical response to the puzzle posed by TVEs has been to label them a "transitional" form of enterprise, adapted to cope with an "underdeveloped" institutional environment. However, while TVEs did in fact eventually decline, their eclipse did not necessarily reflect the operation of a transcendental historical principle, as the discourse of transition suggests. Rather, a series of political decisions made by central state authorities helped precipitate their fall.

Politically, TVEs became victims of their economic success. By the late 1980s the Chinese economy was overheating, due in considerable part to TVEs' phenomenal performance. Faced with a runaway inflation, the central government feared it was losing economic control, and with the Tiananmen Square protests in 1989 also political control. What is more, ever since the reforms began, the state's spending continually exceeded its receipts. To gain and to maintain support for the Four Modernizations—all of which were costly—it had raised both the procurement price it paid for grain it purchased from peasants as well as the wages it paid for its industrial workers in the city.

In order to balance its books, the central government once again restructured the tax and financial sectors. In 1994, it undertook a program of fiscal recentralization with the goal of increasing its tax receipts. As earlier fiscal contracts (*caizhengbaogan*) between the center and provinces, and ultimately between the provinces and their subunits, were redrawn, the center increased its share of tax receipts and reduced that of the lower levels of government. This put severe financial stress on townships and villages in particular. Located at the very bottom of the fiscal food chain, they were now required to pass up more and more of their tax receipts to higher levels of government while remaining responsible for their local welfare expenses.

At the same time the central government undertook a reform of the financial sector. In particular, it cracked down on rural credit, thus depriving the local state of alternative sources of financing at a time when it needed them the most. As more and more rural residents had found employment in TVEs, they had deposited their savings in local financial institutions, which in turn helped support rural industry. As part of its effort to keep urban SOEs afloat, the state now sought to redirect the rural credit boom to cities to help defray SOEs' losses and to finance their restructuring.

Even as the central government was effectively squeezing TVEs out of business, in 1997 it promulgated, for the first time, a national law regulating their establishment and operation.[17] While the new law finally formally spelled out ownership relations in TVEs and set out rules for their internal governance, with the stated goal of "separating government from enterprise" (*zhengqi fenkai*), TVEs continued to decline as an organizational form. Hardin and his followers would have predicted the opposite: Presumably a clarification of TVEs' ownership structure should have helped them *avoid* the tragedy of the commons. In fact, the new law was not so much an elucidation of property rights as part of a larger redefinition of TVEs' role in the political economy of the PRC. It sought to put the genie back in the bottle by turning TVEs into traditional small-scale undertakings by rural collectives, with the

17 Zhonghua Renmin Gongheguo Xiangzhen Qiye Fa [Law of the People's Republic of China on Township Enterprises] (promulgated by the Standing Committee of the National People's Congress Oct. 29, 1996, effective Jan. 1, 1997, repealed Dec. 27, 2025).

limited role of supporting agriculture. Over time these retrofitted TVEs came to be eclipsed by "true" private enterprises that no longer needed to identify publicly as quasi-socialist collectives for purposes of institutional legitimacy.

Remaking the Peasant

By way of conclusion, let us consider China's rural development more systematically in light of the English experience. The return to family farming under the Household Responsibility System was in many ways similar to the first stage of the Enclosure Movement: Both broke up a rural commons into smaller units. However, in China the initial fragmentation of collectively held land was not followed by its reconsolidation into large commercial farms. The reason for this is simple: Unlike in England, property in China's agricultural land was not commodified. In the first stage, only *cultivation* was decollectivized—peasant households were allocated a provisional, nontransferable use right to the land they farmed, while the land itself remained under collective ownership.

As noted above, many observers regard the Household Responsibility System as a transition from socialism to a (partial) market economy, yet it is better understood as a kind of socialist commons that was not unlike the *feudal* commons in England, rather than its capitalist replacement. As we have observed, the feudal commons was marked by a combination of individual and collective elements overlaid on top of another. Most notably, tenants of various kinds possessed strips of land they held individually. Those strips were typically noncontiguous to ensure that everyone got their fair share of both the highest quality fields as well as the poorest ones. In many areas of China, too, households received ten or more noncontiguous strips of collective land, precisely to ensure a fair distribution.

While the Household Responsibility System is often celebrated as "emancipation" of Chinese peasantry, not all peasants were in favor of dividing up communal land into household allotments, or at least not to such an extent as was done. In many cases, pressure for dividing up cultivation came from county officials above. In densely populated areas such as the Yangzi Delta, for example, allocations tended to be small, often barely large enough for subsistence cultivation, much as had been the case after the breakup of the commons in the first stage of the English Enclosure Movement. Moreover, although the system gave each individual household a greater incentive to invest labor in the land it tilled, it also discouraged earlier practices of cooperation. Especially in poorer and less productive regions where collaboration was essential, the division of land was likely to lead to less, rather than more, efficient farming.

Just as many peasants resisted the initial division of land into household allotments, they also objected when these temporary allotments began to be made for longer periods. The first allocations under the Household Responsibility System were limited to three to five years, after which they were subject to review. Over time, the central state began to restrict reallocations, seeking to turn temporary use rights into something more akin to permanent or semipermanent enclosures, eventually as long as thirty years for arable land, to be extended for another thirty years upon expiration.[18] Nearly two-thirds of the farmers studied by the sociologist Jonathan Unger favored the egalitarianism of temporary use rights over more secure ownership.[19] For these cultivators collective security over time was evidently of greater value than a sense of individual ownership.

There is also debate about the extent to which—and even whether—the Household Responsibility System in fact increased agricultural productivity. The bulk of the increase in rural incomes came from the

18 Zhonghua Renmin Gongheguo Nongcun Tudi Chengbao Fa [Rural Land Contracting Law of the People's Republic of China] (promulgated by the Standing Committee of the National People's Congress Aug. 29, 2002, effective Mar. 1, 2003, most recently amended Dec. 29, 2018), article 21, provides for contracting terms of thirty years for arable land, up to fifty years for grassland, and up to seventy years for forest land.

19 Jonathan Unger, *The Transformation of Rural China* (New York: Routledge, 2002), 225.

development of industry. There is little question that agricultural incomes increased as well, but much of that increase was due to the fact that the state raised the price it paid for its grain requisitions, as noted above. The historic challenges of Chinese agriculture have always been the scarcity of land and water, and they remained difficult to overcome. During the Maoist era, the bulk of the increase in agricultural productivity came not from capital investments but from channeling rural labor into transforming the natural landscape itself. After the establishment of the Household Responsibility System, families with small holdings could not afford to invest in mechanized farming. Instead, they increased their yields by turning from reliance on mostly organic fertilizers to the intensive use of chemical ones, which became widely available and affordable as TVEs began to produce them.

Although this provided quick short-term gains, it also degraded the quality of the soil over time and, even worse, turned into a major environmental hazard when fertilizers began to seep into the water supply. Beyond long-term damage to ecology and human health, the introduction of household farming led to social decay as well. With decreasing investments in human capital—namely, education and health—the previous decades' remarkable advancements in rural literacy and health began also to erode.

This deterioration of public infrastructure was accompanied by a decline of a general sense of community. A rural migrant who returned to his home village after a prolonged absence in 1992 complained that the village's entire appearance had changed: "There is no village centre, nor is there a playground for children . . . there is no longer any focal point for public life in the village."[20] Another one bemoaned that even during the Chinese New Year the village was "not as bustling as before. People are not together any more. Only family members spend time together, chat, and visit relatives."[21] Put differently, the new emphasis

20 Harrell, *An Ecological History of Modern China*, 167.

21 Hairong Yan, *New Masters, New Servants: Migration, Development, and Women Workers in China* (Durham, NC: Duke University Press, 2008), 227.

on the household undermined the sense of a village community as a whole, leading to a gradual withdrawal into the domestic sphere.

When viewed in light of these developments, the decollectivization of agriculture did not represent a commodification of either land or labor—the key fictitious commodities signaling the emergence of a market society, in Karl Polanyi's vocabulary. The Household Responsibility System was essentially an administrative scheme for land use allocation that was accompanied by a partial commodification of agricultural products—decidedly "real" commodities—and even their commodification was restricted insofar as a portion of grain continued to be requisitioned by the state at state-mandated prices. Just as this decollectivization did not result in the commodification of land, it also did not entail a general commodification of agricultural labor, as each household was still expected to till its own land.

Just as the process of agricultural decollectivization was similar to as well as different from the parcelization of the English commons, its consequences also both corresponded to and diverged from those of its English counterpart. In both instances the reorganization of agriculture ultimately gave rise to rural industry. In the first phase, the new industry took the form of textile mills in England and TVEs in China, and in China, too, textile industry was one of the first main TVE sectors, relying on largely female labor.

In China's case, however, the establishment of rural industry did not entail a large-scale dispossession. England's early industrialization was premised on a regime of privately owned capital, forged out of the commons, whereas the bulk of Chinese TVEs were collectively owned enterprises. To the extent that a rural collective provided the land, capital, and labor for its industry, the members of the collective evidently did not need to dispossess themselves in order to operate and work in their own enterprises. To be sure, in contrast to the decollectivization of agriculture, rural industrialization did entail a partial commodification of labor. But even the organization of labor was not subject to market principles alone, as evidenced by TVEs' preference for hiring villagers over outsiders and paying the former more than the latter.

Nor is the way in which TVEs combined socialist features with corporate structures as heterodox as it may sound. Marx, for one, believed that a publicly traded corporation in which ownership and management are separated—in contrast to early industrial factories run by private owners—constituted "the abolition of capital as private property within the confines of the capitalist mode of production itself." When private capital is no longer held by an individual owner but by a group of shareholders removed from the actual business of management, private capital becomes "social capital."[22] If even a business corporation could be viewed as "the abolition of the capitalist mode of production within the capitalist mode of production itself," we may think of TVEs as the abolition of the socialist mode of production within the socialist mode of production—an intermediate form without a fully determinate relationship to either capitalism or socialism.

In any event, it is clear that TVEs represented a transformation in the role of the rural state rather than its retreat. As Jean Oi observes, "privatization does not have a monopoly on the capacity to generate growth."[23] The economist Barry Naughton remarks similarly, "in no other transitional economy has public ownership played such a role."[24] There is no question that the decollectivization of agriculture and the rise of rural industry remade the Chinese peasant of the Maoist era: Rather than restricted primarily to cultivation, a peasant could now be a farmer and/or a worker and combine those attributes at various times in various ways, as rural folk had historically done. To the extent that the notion of a Chinese peasant itself was a Maoist invention, it might be tempting to say that the socialist peasant was effectively *un*-made, rather than just remade. That would be an overstatement. With continuing collective ownership and with the household registration system still in place, rural citizens were still tied to land, even as they were increasingly putting that land to nonagricultural uses.

---

22 Karl Marx, *Capital*, vol. 3 (London: Penguin, 1981), 567.

23 Oi, *Rural China Takes Off*, 194.

24 Barry Naughton, "Chinese Institutional Innovation and Privatization from Below," *American Economic Review* 84, no. 2 (1995): 266.

Finally, it is important to consider the combined effects of the decollectivization of agricultural production and the rise of collectively owned rural industry. Despite continuing controls on peasant mobility, the longstanding distinction between city and country began to diminish as industrial labor became increasingly widespread in the countryside. Moreover, as we have seen, many TVEs provided not only employment but also welfare benefits, although those benefits fell short of the iron rice bowl offered by urban SOEs. While the emergence of rural industry may have been an unintended consequence of agricultural reform, its development became a crucial means of alleviating rural poverty.

In sum, the Household Responsibility System was a pragmatic adjustment in the way in which collective land was cultivated that sought to address rural poverty. Although it also gave rise to a burgeoning rural industry that ultimately remade the role of the peasant, it is equally important to appreciate what the reform did not do. It did not entail a general commodification of agricultural land or labor, and peasants continued to be held collectively responsible for their own welfare. Equally importantly, with respect to the urban state-controlled economy, *nothing changed*: Landless workers continued to live off the labor they performed for the state, in contrast to peasants who were still expected to live off the land they owned and tilled. Accordingly, the urban working class continued to be looked after, and looked over, by the state—until they were not.

3

Unmaking the Worker: Urban Proletarianization, 1994–Present

We never forcibly evict anybody, except those who refuse to move.
—Mayor of Beijing, quoted in Yasheng Huang, *Capitalism with Chinese Characteristics*

It is vital to refuse the nearly irresistible tendency to read every aspect of China's post-1978 development as part of capitalism's inevitable unfolding—a propensity often shared by analyses emanating from the left as much as the right. As we have seen, the early phase of the reforms is best understood as an evolution in Chinese socialism. It now remains for us to consider how those reforms have been essential for the emergence of a new state capitalism, even as the new order has undermined them, giving rise to a reconfigured political economy that has transformed the Chinese lifeworld, rural and urban alike.

Looking back, chapter 1 recounted the making of the industrial working class, housed in urban SOEs and subsidized by a peasantry tied to the land. In chapter 2, we saw how the early agrarian reforms destabilized this foundational dichotomy: The decollectivization of agriculture led to the development of TVEs, which gave rise to a growing industrial workforce in the countryside. A hybrid between a commercial enterprise and a socialist collective, a classic TVE provided benefits to the community beyond employment, not unlike an SOE, although TVE benefits varied more from one enterprise to another and were overall less extensive and not guaranteed by the state. While the reformers had not envisioned the rise of TVEs, in the end the reforms accomplished what they sought to do: They reduced the historic welfare gap between an impoverished peasantry and an elite industrial workforce in cities.

This chapter outlines the unmaking of China's working class as a privileged stratum under state socialism. After its deliberate initial focus on the alleviation of rural poverty, in the early 1990s the Party made a decisive turn from rural to urban development. This reorientation ultimately gave birth to a new regime of technocratic state capitalism that transformed China into the economic superpower it is today.

Although the Party-state's decision-making is often opaque, it does not seem that this was the outcome of a detailed and fully thought-out plan. Much as the rise of rural industry had been an unintended byproduct of the fiscal restructuring that took place in 1980, the urban transformation too began with a tax reorganization that turned out to have far-reaching consequences. As we saw in chapter 2, the new round of fiscal restructuring began as an essentially pragmatic response to address the central government's deteriorating finances. Yet even though there may never have existed a master plan for building up a system of state capitalism, there is no question that once it arose it was embraced by the Party leadership and has come to be seen as vital for China's continued economic development and stability.

At the heart of the state's new development agenda was the reorganization of SOEs. It entailed a fundamental restructuring of both industrial capital and industrial labor. First, deficit-ridden state-owned entities were transformed into the legal form of the shareholding corporation, allowing them to acquire non-state capital to help stabilize their finances. So long as the state remained the controlling shareholder, this reorganization changed mostly the form in which the state exercised its control over SOEs. However, this restructuring was accompanied by SOE workers being put on ordinary employment contracts, subject to the vagaries of hiring and firing. This "breaking of the iron rice bowl" revolutionized the state's relationship to labor, with consequences that have cascaded throughout society.

Because of the all-encompassing nature of the SOE work unit, in the end its unwinding has reconfigured the relationship among the state, the family, and the market. It is no exaggeration to say that the unmaking of the Chinese industrial working class has led to the remaking of Chinese society as a whole. It also began again to widen the cleavage between city and country. It is this new regime that became the foundation for the China we see in global media today: megacities with futuristic skylines, funded by global capital and built by armies of migrant labor.

The present chapter focuses on the transformation of urban China and its integration with the global economy. In this new phase, the erstwhile masters of the factory were effectively expropriated of the ownership of their workplaces and transformed into an industrial proletariat in the Marxian sense. However, it is important to observe at the outset that the indirect effects of these urban transformations will ultimately cause a corresponding revolution in the countryside, fusing the remains of China's rural socialism with the institutions of global capitalism.

Classic SOE Work Unit

Let us return briefly to the initial making of the Chinese working class. As we have seen, SOEs were owned by the state, located on state-owned land, and subsidized by the countryside. Theoretically, the workers were the ultimate owners of SOEs—its "masters"—and thus working for themselves rather than performing alienated labor. A classic SOE work unit was the chief vehicle for delivering a privileged material existence to urban industrial workers, providing them with lifetime job security as well as a cradle-to-grave system of welfare, including housing, childcare, schools, hospitals, cultural facilities, and retirement benefits. Effectively, it combined the functions of the state, the market, and the family in a single package.

Legally, as we have seen, an SOE constituted an "industrial enterprise owned by the whole people." The term itself represents an attempt to elide the troublesome distinction between "the people" and "the state." Under this definition, an SOE had little organizational integrity. Part of the state plan, it was simply one administrative unit in the larger national economy—a glorified accounting convention in the calculus of collective benefit. Put differently, even the biggest SOE was only a small subunit of the mother company, which was the People's Republic as a whole. In addition to SOEs, there were smaller collectively owned industrial enterprises in Chinese cities—urban equivalents of the rural agricultural collectives. Both rural and urban collectives were formally outside the state plan. However, in rural collectives peasants were responsible for their own welfare, whereas workers in urban collectives enjoyed access to a range of state-sponsored benefits, although those benefits fell short of what full-fledged SOEs provided.

Although based on the Soviet model, Chinese SOEs varied greatly along several vectors, including their size, the industrial sector in which they operated, and their relative location in the state hierarchy. Originally, they had been envisioned as under direct ministerial supervision, like their Soviet counterparts, but as difficulties of central planning from Beijing became evident, the immediate oversight of numerous SOEs—especially smaller ones in less vital sectors—was delegated to lower levels of government. Different SOEs have therefore been controlled by different levels of state administration, ranging from central ministries to provincial, prefectural, and municipal governments.

While drawing initially on the Soviet model, Mao Zedong came soon to disdain its technocratic orientation, privileging a professional elite of engineers, scientists, and managers. Spurning economic incentives, Mao insisted on the motivational force of ideology. Their differences aside, workers in Chinese SOEs lived a remarkably egalitarian existence. Cadres in Chinese SOEs were paid essentially the same as workers, and they shared the same social space and same living quarters. Nearly all women were employed, although they remained disproportionately responsible for unremunerated domestic labor, as we have seen. Much as TVEs defied successfully the tragedy of the commons, so did SOEs: While cadres might have been expected to hoard assets and opportunities, they were expected to exemplify socialist morality by taking *less* than their fair share, and in fact often did so. While shirking occurred, most workers performed their duties willingly and well.

The work unit was also a site of governance, as we have seen. The state's nearly total control over it helped reduce crime, prostitution, and drug use society-wide. It made it possible to increase the urban population's health and literacy equally dramatically, much as was occurring in the countryside under the aegis of agricultural collectives. The state asserted its control over the labor market as well, replacing it with a unified labor recruitment and allocation system (*tongzhao tongpei*). Under this system, job candidates were assigned administratively to SOEs based on state labor bureaus' assessment of where they were most needed. Contract-based labor continued to exist, but it remained devalued and marginal, by definition the province of temporary workers.

It was technically possible to transfer from one work unit to another, but in practice such transfers were rare. This stability heightened workers' sense of ownership of their workplaces. Officially, workers were encouraged to treat "the factory as family" (*yichang weijia*), and colloquially they often referred to it as "the great family" (*da jiating*). In a literalization of this metaphor, there emerged a widespread practice of children succeeding to their parents' positions upon retirement (*dingti*). Internal recruitment (*neizhao*) was another form of affirmative action for families, allowing work units to hire employees' children even prior to the parents' retirement. When internal recruitment failed to integrate families, SOEs often set up collective enterprises as de facto subsidiaries to employ spouses and other intimates.

Early Reforms

The reorganization of the state economy in the mid-1990s was unprecedented in scope. It was prefigured by a series of more modest reforms, many of which sought to mimic the early rural ones. Structurally an SOE is much like the TVEs that emerged in the early 1980s: a public enterprise with a separation of ownership and management. TVEs were owned collectively by all villagers, making it village officials' job to ensure that they were managed in villagers' interest. Similarly, an SOE was owned by the Chinese people as a whole, and it was the duty of the corresponding ministries, and the bureaucracies under them, to ensure that they were operated for the people's benefit.

Given these parallel structures, in principle the central state should have been in as a good a position as a village to oversee its enterprises, yet the performance of the state sector as a whole fell short of that of TVEs. In fact, SOEs' main problem was not the state's lack of effective oversight over its enterprises but rather it having *too much* control. In contrast to the relative autonomy and organizational simplicity of the rural state, the central state is made up of numerous overlapping bureaucracies and agencies. Consequently, SOE managers were subject to intensive monitoring by multiple bureaucracies with inconsistent and often contradictory interests, each seeking to use the enterprises under its supervision to its own advantage—a phenomenon characterized colloquially as having "too many mothers-in-law" (*popo duo*).[1]

To address this problem, the ubiquitous catchphrase in the early stages of SOE restructuring was "enterprise autonomy." In the first place, this stood for enacting a genuine functional separation between ownership and management in order to relieve SOE managers from excessive and inconsistent control. Secondly, it was a call for recognizing SOEs as legal persons in their own right. Rendering them distinct from the rest of the state apparatus held the promise of relieving the state from its ultimate responsibility for SOEs' deficits. The goal was to create enterprises that functioned economically like business corporations yet continued to be owned by the public. This was precisely the feat that TVEs had managed to accomplish as a hybrid organizational form.

But how were SOEs to be provided with greater autonomy? An early response was another extension of the contract responsibility system beyond agricultural households and intra-governmental fiscal contracting, namely the establishment of a so-called contract management responsibility system (*chengbao jingying zeren zhi*). Under this system,

1 Donald C. Clarke, "Regulation and Its Discontents: Understanding Economic Law in China," *Stanford Journal of International Law* 28, no. 2 (1992): 293.

the day-to-day management of SOEs was contracted to professional managers, much as was done in TVEs. Depending on the terms of the arrangement, managers were obligated to submit a certain amount of the SOE's proceeds to the state while retaining a right to all or part of any residual, the specifics varying from enterprise to enterprise. Furthermore, while SOEs continued to be subject to state planning, they were also allowed to produce things outside the plan so long as they met their mandatory targets, much like rural households were allowed to produce for the market once they met their quotas. The goal was to improve efficiency while encouraging the production of consumer goods and other commodities neglected in the state plan.

Seeking to realize this vision, a new Industrial Enterprise Law enacted in 1988 stated unambiguously that an SOE was an independent legal person with a right to control its own assets and liable for its own debts. An Enterprise Bankruptcy Law had already been enacted in 1986. Together, these two laws provided for the ultimate possibility of the liquidation of SOEs whose liabilities exceeded their assets. At the same time, the state discontinued the practice of extracting SOE earnings simply as rents and began to tax their profits instead. These enactments sought to transform SOEs, by legislative fiat, from a political arm of the state into essentially economic entities. However, these reforms were undermined by other practices. The Enterprise Bankruptcy Law remained mostly a symbolic warning to bad managers as hardly any SOEs were allowed to go bankrupt. Simultaneously, while the state was no longer directly responsible for SOEs' liabilities, state-owned banks continued to provide financing to insolvent enterprises in the form of "policy loans" that had few prospects of being repaid. The policies justifying these loans were entirely understandable in the context of China's political economy as a whole. Permitting insolvent SOEs to go bankrupt would have resulted in mass unemployment. That was simply not acceptable in the absence of both an extensive labor market and general social security institutions beyond the work unit.

The reforms altered also labor's relationship to their supervisors. The socialist factory director (*gongzhang*) was transformed into a general manager (*zong jingli*). Workers began to be offered material incentives, including higher wages and bonuses. This represented a sea change. The classic Chinese SOE had functioned well within its socialist logic until the introduction of market institutions began to undermine it. When all workers had stood on the same plane, cadres had no choice but to rely on persuasion and leadership by example in order to motivate workers to meet their production targets. Indeed, many workers were dismayed by the new economic inequality, objecting to even modest disparities in pay.[2] At same time, as managers gained more power and that power became increasingly personal, they found themselves in a position to issue orders and dispense favors. Remarkably, shirking became widespread *after* the introduction of material rewards. In the absence of effective oversight, corruption and clientelism emerged as systemic problems.

These early reforms of the state sector paled in significance to what was happening outside of it. SOEs' viability was undermined critically by the advent of a range of new competitors, beyond the rural collective economy represented by booming TVEs: Chinese private enterprises and foreign private enterprises. They emerged along separate trajectories under distinctive ideological and structural constraints. As part of the Household Responsibility System, the state had recognized early on an indigenous form of enterprise called an "individual household" (*getihu*), essentially a small-scale family business. It was permitted both in cities and in the countryside, and eventually it became a one-size-fits-all template for all manner of petty capitalist enterprises. The number of outside employees in these household entities was capped by law at seven, on the theory that a greater reliance on commodified labor would turn what was essentially a family enterprise into an ideologically suspect private firm in the proper sense of the

2 See, for example, Joel Andreas, *Disenfranchised: The Rise and Fall of Industrial Citizenship in China* (Oxford: Oxford University Press, 2019), 189; Huaiyin Li, *The Master in Bondage: Factory Workers in China 1949–2019* (Stanford, CA: Stanford University Press, 2023), 115.

term. (The seemingly arbitrary cap derived from an anecdote in Marx's *Capital* in which the exemplary capitalist employs eight workers.[3]) In fact, entrepreneurs ignored the restriction with dazzling impunity, hiring dozens—even hundreds—of employees, stretching traditional fictions of kinship-based households to their breaking point, and beyond. In 1988, the state finally promulgated Provisional Regulations on Private Enterprises, which legalized private enterprises employing more than eight workers.

The legalization of foreign investment likewise proceeded by stages. It began hesitantly, limited geographically at first to so-called Special Economic Zones, with the primary goal of obtaining foreign technology. It was initially restricted to joint ventures with TVEs and SOEs and later expanded to include joint ventures with privately owned Chinese enterprises. Wholly foreign-owned enterprises were finally authorized in 1986. Their varied histories and features aside, these new forms of Chinese and foreign enterprise were similar in one key respect: They employed commodified labor, with few obligations to their workers beyond the timely payment of wages—although remarkably often they failed to meet even this basic obligation.

Barry Naughton has famously described the gradual evolution of China's economy as "growing out of the plan."[4] However, at least as far as SOEs are concerned, they did not so much outgrow socialism as found themselves engulfed on all sides by an ever-rising tide of market institutions. Instructively, the colloquial term for leaving the security of the state sector for private enterprise is "jumping into the ocean" (*xiahai*). The commodification of labor, like so many other reforms, was initially segmented, partial, and gradual, but once it spread beyond the Special Economic Zones and across the various enterprise forms, SOEs'

3 Xu Qingquan. "Siying jingji shi zenme huode zhunshengzheng de [How do private businesses obtain licences]?," *Beijing ribao* [Beijing Daily], April 20, 2007. Cf. Karl Marx, *Capital*, vol. 1 (London: Penguin Classics, 1992), 423.

4 See Barry Naughton, *Growing Out of the Plan: Chinese Economic Reform, 1978–1993* (Cambridge: Cambridge University Press, 1995).

existence became increasingly impossible—a phenomenon the labor scholar Mary Gallagher characterizes as "contagious capitalism."[5]

Restructuring Capital: The Global Turn

The restructuring of the state economy marked a shift not only from agricultural development to state-led urban industrialization but also a turn toward global capital with global consequences. This reversal of economic strategy was highly contested. The rural boom of the 1980s had resulted in inflation which helped fuel the Tiananmen protests in 1989. Together, they triggered a conservative backlash. The tide did not turn again until Deng Xiaoping's legendary Southern Tour in 1992 to the city of Shenzhen (notably modeled on imperial progresses by Ming and Qing rulers), which paid homage to the village-turned-economic-juggernaut just outside of Hong Kong.

Deng famously advocated that "to get rich is glorious." Simultaneously, he also urged to "let some people get rich first." His was an unapologetic brand of socialism with economic development as the overriding goal and equality a distant second behind an ever-receding horizon. Squaring this with orthodox Marxism required temporal adjustments in the operation of the laws of historical materialism. The new reforms came to be justified ideologically by the claim that the PRC was in "the primary stage of socialism" (*shehuizhuyi chuji jieduan*). By implication, unless and until China arrived at its final socialist destination, capitalist elements would continue to be part of its economy. Socialism's peaceful coexistence with capitalism was sanctioned under the new rubric of "socialist market economy" (*shehuizhuyi shichang jingji*). Admittedly, it was difficult to pin down what exactly a socialist market economy *was*—it sounded rather like squaring the circle—but therein lay the term's utility. The new concept was codified in the Constitution in 1993, the year that a new, pathbreaking round of SOE reforms began.

5 See Mary Gallagher, *Contagious Capitalism: Globalization and the Politics of Labor in China* (Princeton, NJ: Princeton University Press, 2007).

That same year, the PRC also promulgated its first-ever Company Law, effective as of 1994. Insofar as the business corporation is the quintessential form of enterprise under capitalism, the very enactment of the law was a major ideological event. In practice, however, the Company Law was less than revolutionary. In many regards, it was an attempt to catch up with practices that had emerged even in the absence of legal authorization. Many TVEs had been raising capital by issuing shares since the early 1980s, organizing themselves as "shareholder cooperative enterprises" (*gufen hezuo qiye*). At first, shares were offered only to employees. In many ways they were more akin to fixed-income securities, yet over time they became increasingly transferable. Soon lower-level SOEs began to imitate TVEs. As early as 1986, the number of enterprises issuing shares had reached 6,000 to 7,000 nationwide, giving birth to over-the-counter markets for enterprise shares in several major cities. By 1990 even large SOEs in major cities were issuing shares to the public, lack of legal sanction notwithstanding.[6]

Despite the conservative post-Tiananmen reaction, the state had little choice but to recognize the fact that there existed an active securities market. It established a stock exchange in Shanghai in 1990 and another one in Shenzhen in 1991. However, rather than slaying a rising "stock fever," the regularization of stock markets only fed the rage for speculation, sparking a major riot at the Shenzhen Stock Exchange in 1992—the most serious unrest the country had seen since the Tiananmen protests. The new Company Law was part of a larger effort to bring order to capital markets by standardizing the way in which struggling SOEs harnessed outside capital.

6 See Carl F. Walter and Fraser J. T. Howie, *Privatizing China: Inside China's Stock Markets* (Singapore: John Wiley & Sons, 2006), 67–8. Lynn White describes a shareholding boom in 1987, with several large SOEs raising capital by selling stock, mostly to workers, resulting in the State Council prohibiting issuance of shares without permission. Lynn White, *Unstately Power, vol. 1: Local Causes of China's Economic Reforms* (Armonk, NY: M. E. Sharpe, 1998), 323.

In contrast to what was happening in postsocialist Eastern Europe at the time, China's turn to private capital was never envisioned as an outright privatization (*siyouhua*), which remained anathema for political as well as economic reasons. Rather, the reform was characterized as a "corporatization" (*gongsihua*) of SOEs. It was not intended to abolish the fundamental ideological and constitutional principle of state ownership of the means of production. Rather, it was designed to alter primarily the legal form that public ownership takes. Even in corporatized SOEs, the state would remain the controlling shareholder. At the same time, by providing for ownership in commodified shares—in lieu of an undivided and nontransferable ownership held by the state on behalf of "the whole people"—the Company Law blessed SOEs with the authority to raise new capital to help them compete with their private competitors.

In effect, the state turned away from its reliance on primitive socialist accumulation—the coercive transfer of rural resources—to the ordinary technologies of financial capitalism, namely, raising money on capital markets. This reorientation gave SOEs potential access to global sources of financing as well. The state had learned that relying on domestic capital had its own risks. When publicly listed SOEs performed poorly, aggrieved retail investors were liable to take to the streets, holding the state responsible. Utilizing global capital allowed the state to export any potential social turmoil caused by the performance of its corporatized SOEs: No matter how disappointed they might be, unhappy foreign investors posed little risk to domestic stability.

Yet overall, these reforms did not lead to marked improvements in SOEs' governance. To the extent that a corporatized SOE is a hybrid—much like its rural cousin, the TVE—it too is part commercial enterprise, part socialist commons. Internally, it is structured in the hierarchical form of a corporation, yet externally it is expected to serve the interests of "the whole people." A paradigmatic TVE, however, was grounded literally in a village commons and the supporting institutions. The relatively weak performance of corporatized SOEs raises the question of whether there exists an effective *national* commons as well, with corresponding institutions of accountability. Just as TVEs took on the institutional form of the local state, a reorganized SOE was essentially an administrative unit of the central state that was reconstituted as a corporate bureaucracy. However, SOEs' relatively weak economic record suggests that the central state is less accountable to "the people" than village institutions are to villagers' interests. The New Left critic Wang Hui attributes the difficulties of SOE regulation specifically to a lack of democratic governance on the national level, in contrast to relatively egalitarian village institutions.[7]

SOEs, however, form a diverse group, and some have in fact been more successful than others. Understanding the operation of public enterprise in the PRC requires ultimately a fine-grained, even anthropological, analysis of the state, not only in the case of rural institutions of local governance but also with respect to the institutions of the central state. Precisely because the state is not a singular entity, *where* an enterprise is located in the administrative hierarchy of the state can be as significant as the form of ownership in which it is organized. There is empirical evidence suggesting that the state's efforts to reform SOEs in the 1980s and early 1990s were more successful in the case of entities that were managed by lower levels of government—urban analogues of rural enterprises managed by townships and villages.

Insofar as one of the main challenges has been creating *greater* distance between the state and SOEs, this may seem counterintuitive. By definition, provincial and city governments are more intimately involved with the entities under their jurisdiction than faraway central ministries. One might therefore expect that these entities would be especially vulnerable to negative "interference" by their official overseers. Yet it seems that at least in some cases it is precisely supervisory officials' proximity to their enterprises that has contributed to lower-level entities' success. Much as was the case with many rural TVEs, the sociologist Doug Guthrie's study of urban enterprises found it frequently difficult to distinguish a lower-level city government from the entities under its jurisdiction,

7 Wang Hui, *The End of Revolution: China and the Limits of Modernity* (Cambridge, MA: Harvard University Press, 2009), 25.

leading him to conclude that these governments functioned like holding companies, providing governance and oversight to their enterprises as needed. In contrast to struggling higher-level SOEs with greater autonomy, he found that it was generally low-level enterprises, except for those at the very bottom, that "have been better at transforming themselves."[8] Again, it should probably not surprise us that one thing that government can provide is governance, even if its extent and quality varies from one level to the next.

Perhaps unexpectedly, the Company Law turned out to be highly useful for private enterprises, too, despite the fact that its primary purpose was to provide a new legal foundation for the state sector—or, ironically, because of that fact. Throughout the 1980s and mid-1990s private enterprise had been in search of organizational forms that would destigmatize it ideologically, beyond the limited model of the household-based family business (*getihu*). The available legal forms remained politically suspect precisely because they were limited *exclusively* to private owners. This stigma was a major reason why entrepreneurs were more numerous in the countryside than in cities through the mid-1990s: Already consigned to an inferior social rank without access to the job and welfare privileges of their urban counterparts, rural entrepreneurs were more willing to take on the demeaned status associated with private enterprise and the official discrimination against it. The main alternative, as we saw in chapter 2, was to don a "red hat" and to camouflage one's business as a collective enterprise.

Even though the primary purpose of the new Company Law was to restructure the state sector, for the first time it offered a legal form that was available to *all* actors—public as well private, urban as well as rural, Chinese as well as foreign. In terms of jurisprudence, this was a major milestone toward creating a unified legal system. In practical terms, after the corporatization of SOEs an outside observer has no obvious way of telling whether an enterprise incorporated under the Company Law is

8 Doug Guthrie, *Dragon in a Three-Piece Suit: The Emergence of Capitalism in China* (Princeton, NJ: Princeton University Press, 1999), 208.

ultimately owned by the state or held privately. This has afforded private entrepreneurs a kind of legitimacy that earlier legal forms for exclusively private enterprise never could. Even a private enterprise can gain an identity as a "public corporation" of sorts by selling shares to the public, taking advantage of Marx's observation that insofar as private capital becomes available to the public it becomes "social capital."

Restructuring Labor: Expropriating the Worker

Most students of SOE reform focus on corporate governance. In legal scholarship in particular, the organization of capital belongs to the purview of those who study corporation law and securities law while the organization of labor is the province of employment law and labor law. Yet it is simply not possible to understand the implications of the restructuring of state capital without also considering its consequences for labor, much as one must consider city and country in relation to one another. Whereas the corporatization of SOEs changed primarily the form in which state exercises its control over capital—as an investor rather than outright owner—it ended up utterly transforming the state's relationship to labor.

In conjunction with the promulgation of the Company Law in 1994, China enacted a new Labor Law as well. It required, for the first time, that *all* employers—regardless of their form of ownership—must enter into employment contracts with their workers. While this may sound progressive—and for many workers in the private sector it was, at least potentially—for SOE workers it was a disaster. *This requirement constituted the legal unmaking of the Chinese working class*, in the socialist sense of a stratum of workers who enjoyed a range of privileges by virtue of being employed by an SOE. It marked the official end of lifetime job security with attendant benefits, and it rendered the administrative job allocation system redundant. This was a truly revolutionary development—or a counterrevolutionary one, from a Marxian perspective. What made it all the more remarkable was the fact that it was a revolution by the Chinese *state* against its workers.

The commodification of labor has been without doubt one of the most stupendous aspects of China's post-1978 transformation, along with the commodification of land (discussed below). Although it was instituted gradually across different enterprise forms, it occurred in essentially one generation. Its legalization began sectorally with private and foreign enterprises, as we have seen. With SOEs, it finally arrived at the ideological and economic core of the People's Republic. The introduction of wage labor has changed fundamentally the meaning of work, and even what it means to be a working being. As the labor sociologist Ching Kwan Lee observes, the construction of a market for labor has entailed "a radical reformulation of the mode of domination, political subjectivity, social relations, morality, and notions of time and space."[9]

The social as well psychological significance of the institution of employment contract can hardly be overstated. Just as the Company Law sought to reconstitute SOEs as formally autonomous market actors, the institution of the employment contract does the same on the level of the individual, formalizing the alienation of the worker from the means of production. When SOE employees are put on contracts, the ideological unity of capital and labor is broken and "the people" are atomized into independent economic subjects. Contract establishes the worker as a free agent who agrees to the conditions of his employment—it is a technology of "manufacturing consent," in sociologist Michael Burawoy's phrase.[10] In contrast to the more or less coercive cultivation of socialist unity in an SOE, the employment contract has been aptly described as an "anti-solidarity machine," making each worker individually responsible for his or her own welfare outside of work.[11]

---

9 Ching Kwan Lee, *Against the Law: Labor Protests in China's Rustbelt and Sunbelt* (Los Angeles: University of California Press, 2007), 34.

10 See Michael Burawoy, *Manufacturing Consent: Changes in the Labor Process Under Monopoly Capitalism* (Chicago: University of Chicago Press, 1979).

11 Ching Kwan Lee and Yuan Shen, "An Anti-Solidarity Machine? Labor Non-governmental Organizations in China," in Sarosh Kuruvilla, Ching

Remarkably, many who might have been thought to favor the contractualization of employment resisted it. Even after they became mandatory, numerous SOE managers continued to regard employment contracts as formalities only and insisted on treating their employees as members of a community that produces not only goods but also social security. As one manager reported, while it might be appropriate to make new workers sign contracts, it would not be fair to make old workers do so: "Suddenly to put these people on labor contracts would be cruel. Suddenly they would have no retirement security; that would be very unfair to them . . . It's no way to treat people who have been working for you for so long." When another manager was instructed to focus on profits, she stated flatly, "I don't *do* profits [*wo buzuo lirun*]. My goal is to raise the living standards of my employees." Not unlike a local official in charge of a TVE that returns its profits to the community in the form of public goods, she summed up her policy, "So when we have an excess, I usually just reinvest some of the money in the factory and distribute the rest evenly among the employees."[12]

Although the state first rejected the outright privatization of urban industry, by the late 1990s SOEs found themselves increasingly besieged by TVEs and private enterprises. In 1997, the state adopted a policy of "grasping the large, letting go of the small" (*zhuada, fangxiao*), or selling off small and medium-sized SOEs. Importantly, though, the state has retained its ownership in so-called National Champions, or companies representing "the commanding heights" of China's industry, which is the Leninist phrase conventionally used to characterize them. As the term National Champion suggests, these companies' task is to safeguard the larger national interest, not merely maximize short-term profits. Altogether the state sector still makes up approximately 40 percent of

Kwan Lee, and Mary Gallagher, eds., *From Iron Rice Bowl to Informalization: Markets, Workers, and the State in a Changing China* (Ithaca, NY: Cornell University Press, 2011).

12 Guthrie, *Dragon in a Three-Piece Suit*, 204.

China's gross national product.[13] With respect to the struggling smaller SOEs it chose to sell, the state avoided the ideologically charged term privatization, referring to the process euphemistically as "ownership transformation" (*suoyouzhi gaizao*). That transformation took many forms, ranging from mergers with, and takeovers by, private enterprises to management buyouts. Regardless of their form, these privatizations typically led to or were preceded by mass layoffs, with tens of millions of workers losing their jobs. At the same time, many of the smaller SOEs that survived privatization were allowed go bankrupt. Between the mid-1990s and 2002, employment in the state sector fell by more than a third.[14]

Many industrial workers responded to their layoffs with what Lee describes as "protests of desperation."[15] They recognized that any kind of "large-scale mass incident" (*da guimo qunti shijian*) strikes terror at every Chinese official's heart far more effectively than a lawsuit ever could. These protests were about much more than the prospect of unemployment. To the extent that workers regarded themselves as the masters of the factory, privatization constituted an illegitimate expropriation of their ownership of the workplace, or at least a forced sale of their stake at bargain prices.

To be sure, a classic SOE was formally owned by the state—albeit on behalf of the people—and in strictly legal terms the workers were state employees. However, because of the extraordinary stability of employment in SOEs and the expectation that one would work and die in the same work unit, workers developed a keen sense of ownership in their jobs and the factories in which they toiled. Effectively, an enterprise represented the accumulation of workers' labor, a monument to their willingness to sacrifice for socialism in return for material security. Hence, the workers experienced their dismissal as the expropriation of

13 Raffaele Sciortino, *The US–China Rift and Its Impact on Globalisation: Crisis, Strategy, Transitions* (Chicago: Haymarket Books, 2025), 135.

14 Mark W. Frazier, "State-Sector Shrinkage and Workforce Reduction in China," *European Journal of Political Economy* 22, no. 2 (2006): 435–51.

15 See Ching Kwan Lee, *Against the Law*, 36–125.

their collectively owned property. As one SOE employee put it, "Every inch of grass and every piece of steel in the factory belonged to us workers. They were our sweat and labor . . . These officials just squandered them."[16]

The one area of law to which workers might have looked for support—namely, labor law—is structurally biased again them. The reform-era Constitution, promulgated in 1982 and still in effect, abolished the right to strike, which had been part of the preceding Constitution enacted in 1978. Today, strikes are neither formally prohibited nor legally authorized, and the state has in fact allowed them to take place strategically when it is in its interest to do so. Remarkably, there was no formal employment law until 1994. By definition none was needed in a system in which workers were, in legal theory if not in fact, the owners of the means of production. To this day, there is a single officially recognized union, the All-China Federation of Trade Unions (ACFTU), which is a de-facto extension of the Party-state. In state-controlled enterprises the ACFTU is effectively a representative of the interests of the employer. Strikingly, even in private enterprises the ACFTU branch is regularly coopted by management, to the point that many private employers *welcome* its presence as a co-enforcer of workplace discipline.

Reorganizing Family, Market, and State

As the social contract of lifetime job security has been replaced with the regular employment contract, work has been in effect desocialized as well as depoliticized, and the moral economy of the work unit demoralized. In Gallagher's phrase, "Competition, insecurity, and individual responsibility are the new slogans of the state in its attempt to remake workers to fit the market."[17] Suddenly, the individual confronts the world on his own, responsible for all his needs, starting with such critical questions as where to live, and how. In Michel Foucault's

16 Ibid., 99.

17 Gallagher, *Contagious Capitalism*, 153.

characterization of the subject of neoliberalism, the individual becomes an entrepreneur—an entrepreneur of himself and of living, a combination of human capital and labor power that one must manage for oneself.[18] Depending on one's health, wealth, educational opportunities, and other personal and material resources, those who are able to command higher wages become part of a propertied bourgeoisie, while those with little or no human capital and few resources to build it up are reduced to pure labor.

When a classic socialist SOE is reimagined and restructured as a business corporation, even with the state as the controlling shareholder, massive social consequences follow. The workplace becomes just that—a place for work—rather than a combination of factory, home, school, hospital, and retirement community all rolled into one. With the breakdown of the socialist SOE, social welfare benefits that were previously delivered by the work unit must be provided through other means—either through markets (as housing and much of healthcare are in the PRC today), or directly by the state (for example, basic education), or by the family (for example, childcare). The consequences of SOE reform have thus cascaded across numerous institutions, reconfiguring the entire social, and indeed psychic, landscape of the PRC, and, as the next chapter elaborates, the global landscape as well.

In the first place, the separation of work from family has entailed the transformation of housing from an entitlement to a commodity. Although urban land remains, and must remain, state-owned for ideological reasons, it has been de facto commodified. This has been made possible by creating a market in use rights, distinct from the state's continuing right to ownership—a radical development enshrined in a constitutional amendment in 1998. Even under the new regime, use rights continue to be allocated to state-owned and public entities at no cost or for a nominal fee, and with no time limit. However, under the terms of the Land Administration Law use rights can also be conveyed

18 Michel Foucault, *The Birth of Biopolitics: Lectures at the Collège de France, 1978–1979* (New York: Picador, 2010).

to private entities for periods up to seventy years. The cost of obtaining such rights can be determined either through an auction among several bidders or by negotiating with a potential buyer. In practice, most use rights to urban land have been transferred to commercial entities at negotiated prices, leaving much room for corruption. Insofar as such sales take place at below-market prices, they are in effect a socialist subsidy to private capital.

At first glance, the conveyance of urban land use rights may seem analogous to Household Responsibility System in the countryside, under which the collective maintains its ownership over land but allocates its use to households. However, rural household allocations can only be made to village households, and they are entitlements. A household does not pay the collective to use its plot. Even more importantly, unlike rural use rights under the Household Responsibility System, the right to use urban land is *transferable* and can be bought and sold in secondary markets.

Hence, urban land use rights have not only a use value but an exchange value as well. To be sure, it is only the use right that has been commodified, not land "itself," but this is essentially a metaphysical and legal fiction: What legal ownership of land *means* is precisely the right to use it and to prevent others from doing so. The fact that the state retains the formal ownership of the land has evidently not prevented the emergence of a robust real estate market. One of its main drivers has been the dismantling of the work unit and the consequent demand for private housing. This is an urban form of enclosure that transforms collective housing into private homes, often quite literally into gated communities.

Just as the commodification of industrial labor has led to protests, the transformation of publicly owned housing into a commodity has roused intense resistance. When use rights are sold to developers, many occupants refuse to relocate. Not infrequently, officials have responded by sending out demolition crews to harass protesters and to force out those who remain. Such incidents have turned ordinary people into heroes, symbolized by so-called nail houses (*dingzihu*): singular structures left standing amid flattened construction sites as the occupants refuse to vacate them, sticking out a like nail.[19]

Whereas the work unit of an SOE was a site of both production and consumption, the new urban household is primarily a locus of consumption. Beyond housing, what it does not receive from the state, it must obtain through other means, from food to clothing to childcare. The state has sought to replace some of the social security once offered by the work unit with a new regime of social security legislation. The bulk of the new initiatives—notably, unemployment insurance, health insurance, and retirement benefits—are social insurance programs premised on self-responsibility: They are funded by contributions from individual taxpayers and their employers. Although many of these insurance schemes are mandatory, in the absence of effective oversight numerous employers have failed to offer or to contribute to health care and retirement accounts. Moreover, the regime remains highly fragmented as most social security funds are operated by local governments. Because of the starkly uneven nature of economic development, the poorest areas with the greatest demand for social security programs are in turn also the least likely to be able to fund them.

To make up for such gaps, the state is increasingly turning to family law as a way of privatizing what were previously SOE responsibilities for the poor, the sick, and the old. This development is certainly not unique to China. Reliance on family is one of the main forms of ongoing primitive accumulation on which capitalism depends everywhere. As we have seen, one of the avowed purposes of the all-encompassing socialist work unit was to displace traditional notions of patriarchal kinship and to replace them with a radical egalitarianism—an ethos of everyone "eating from the same pot" to be shared by rural communes and urban SOEs alike.

While women remained primarily responsible for household labor even during the Maoist period, it is ironic that the state is now actively

19 See Teemu Ruskola, *Legal Orientalism: China, the United States, and Modern Law* (Cambridge, MA: Harvard University Press, 2013), 211–13.

promoting the kinds of traditional kinship obligations it once vilified. For example, the Civil Code mandates duties for children to maintain indigent parents and even grandparents, and for siblings to support each other when their parents are unable to do so. Likewise, while it provides for testamentary freedom, it explicitly prohibits testators from disinheriting poor family members and other needy dependents, whether they are related or not.[20] In the same vein, the Law for the Protection of Rights and Interests of the Elderly not only requires that "the elderly shall be provided for mainly by their families," but it even seeks to legislate filial piety more broadly, requiring that children visit their aging parents.[21]

Paradoxically, even as the corporatization of SOEs and other market reforms have made it increasingly vital for the family to re-assume its former social responsibilities, the same reforms have undermined it as a solidary kinship group. In Confucian ideology, the family is an intergenerational unit based on the father-son connection—indeed a kind of corporate entity that is expected to care for its entire membership, as chapter 2 suggested. It was precisely this sense of reciprocal obligation

20 Zhonghua Renmin Gongheguo Minfadian [Civil Code of the People's Republic of China] (promulgated by the National People's Congress of the People's Republic of China May 28, 2020, effective Jan. 1, 2021), articles 1067, 1074–5, 1141. See also Zhonghua Renmin Gongheguo Hunyin Fa [Marriage Law of the People's Republic of China] (promulgated by the Standing Committee of the National People's Congress Sep. 10, 1980, amended Apr. 29, 2001, repealed Jan. 1, 2021), articles 21, 28–9; and Zhonghua Renmin Gongheguo Jicheng Fa [Law of Succession of the People's Republic of China] (promulgated by the National People's Congress of the People's Republic of China Apr. 10, 1985, effective Oct. 1, 1985, repealed Jan. 1, 2021), article 19.

21 Zhonghua Renmin Gongheguo Laonianren Quanyi Baozhang Fa [Law of the People's Republic of China on Protection of the Rights and Interests of the Elderly] (promulgated by the Standing Committee of the National People's Congress Aug. 29, 1996, effective Oct. 1, 1996, most recently amended Dec. 29, 2018), articles 13, 18. See also Civil Code of the People's Republic of China, art. 1067.

that allowed it to become the master metaphor for life in a socialist work unit. Today, this expansive notion of kinship is under stress from the same market institutions that make its survival both indispensable and impossible. Simply in terms of physical space, after the dismantling of work units most families cannot afford dwellings large enough to house multiple generations, contributing to a general decline of intergenerational solidarity.

Simultaneously, the stability of the marital bond has eroded. As the anthropologist Yan Yunxiang describes the changing ideological foundations of the family, it has come to be seen less as a vertical tie between generations and more as a horizontal partnership between husband and wife, premised on the gratification of personal desire.[22] This turn from kinship hierarchy to conjugal partnership in fact parallels the contractualization of the employment relationship, and we should perhaps not be surprised that rising layoffs have been accompanied by rising rates of divorce. The parallel transformations in the organization of the market, the workplace, and the family are a crucial part of a larger reconfiguration of subjectivity.

Finally, the state's one-child policy has further undermined the intergenerational bargain between parents and children. It is increasingly evident that a cohort of only children will not be prepared to support their aging parents, either materially or psychologically. Although the one-child policy has been repealed, it has already produced a generation of young men and women who are individualistic in their outlook, motivated to an unprecedented degree by the satisfaction of personal desire in their economic as well as intimate lives. Indeed, today the two chief arenas for the expression and gratification of private desire are commodities and sex, signaling a decisive shift away from the socialist demand for material sacrifice and emotional loyalty to the Party-state.

---

22 See Yunxiang Yan, *Private Life Under Socialism: Love, Intimacy, and Family in a Chinese Village, 1949–1999* (Stanford, CA: Stanford University Press, 2003).

Proletarianization Under State Capitalism

Having charted the outlines of the unmaking of the Chinese working class, let us return to the English comparison. The genesis of the English proletariat lay in the dispossession of peasants, with the countryside becoming ultimately a source of both industrial capital and industrial labor. In China, the Maoist state had already built an industrial base, also through exactions from the peasantry—albeit not by expropriating their land but, on the contrary, by tying them to it, as we saw in chapter 1. One of the central questions posed by this book is why the state nonetheless has decided to proceed with the expropriation of the peasantry. However, we should pause to ask an analytically and chronologically prior query: Given China's success in setting up an industrial labor force without dispossessing rural cultivators, why proceed to expropriate its *urban* state workers of their jobs, given that both industrial capital and an industrial labor force were already in existence?

The answer is ultimately political rather than economic. Before the reforms, the urban economy was structured in the form of state socialism. From a comparative perspective, the nature of this economy was ambiguous, not unlike the agricultural sector analyzed in chapter 1. On the one hand, when viewed as a whole, we can liken the state sector to a vast industrial enclosure, owned and operated by the state as a super-landlord. On the other hand, we might think of state industry an extended industrial commons belonging to the people. Both characterizations are partly accurate. As we have seen, the Chinese state bureaucracy is in fact not a unified whole. At least on the lower levels, there exist administrative pockets of what we might call sub-commons—local structures that may not be as well-integrated as a rural village but possess a relative degree of local autonomy and an associated set of shared interests and collective norms.

In any event, as we have seen, the state sector was certainly internally coherent enough for several decades, given that it grew at a healthy average rate of 6 percent per year from 1949 to 1978. The unmaking of the socialist working class in the 1990s reflected above all a political reorientation from state socialism to state capitalism. After the state sector was made to compete with private enterprise, it found itself at an insurmountable structural disadvantage, given its obligations not only to maximize output but also to account for its workers' welfare. After the state expropriated industrial workers of their permanent tenure and associated benefits, they became a proletariat in the capitalist sense: a class possessing no property and thus reduced to selling its labor to the highest bidder. Indeed, the Marxian term "proletariat" is rendered into Chinese as *wuchanzhe*—literally, "the propertyless." It is this attribute that distinguishes the expropriated urban workers from the struggling peasants who at least own the land they cultivate, their relative poverty notwithstanding.

The commodification of industrial labor reversed not only the economic fortunes of the Chinese working class but transvalued its public standing as well. Dignity of labor has been one of the chief casualties of SOE reform. Much as capitalism transformed penury from a Christian badge of holiness to one of social shame in Europe, in China, too, poverty has evolved from a political virtue to a moral stain. Under Mao, factory workers stood at the apex of the ideological hierarchy. Though the figurative masters of the factory were not rich, they certainly did not experience their work as dishonorable. In the words of an older worker, "In society, the status of workers was very high. Today, if you say you're a worker, you feel like you're lower than other people."[23] There is no better symbol of this moral reversal than the Party's decision in 2001 to admit millionaires into its membership. If "to get rich is glorious"—and apparently socialist too—then being poor becomes a humiliation.

Unsurprisingly, expropriated Chinese workers responded to their plight much as dispossessed English peasants did. E. P. Thompson outlined two distinct subpolitical traditions of the English working class: rioting and invoking a discourse of the Englishman's birthright.[24]

---

23 Andreas, *Disenfranchised*, 218.

24 E. P. Thompson, *The Making of the English Working Class* (New York: Vintage Books, 1996), 498.

Chinese workers deployed both strategies, frequently combining them. To be sure, rather than appealing to an ancient Anglo-Saxon constitution, laid-off Chinese state workers cited the promises of socialism, demanding their due as heirs to the revolution. Their recollections of life in prereform SOEs may be nostalgic, much as the English myth of a "golden age of village community" before enclosure was, yet, as Thompson observed, "to say it was a 'myth' is not to say it was all false"—even if summoning that past has failed as a strategy more often than it has succeeded.[25]

It is instructive to contrast China's experience with postsocialist reforms in the Soviet Union as well. Crucially, China's transformation is not, and does not present itself as, a postsocialist condition. On the contrary, China today is arguably a *pre*socialist formation in that it purports to be in "the primary stage of socialism." Even if we choose to characterize its economy as a form of capitalism, it is a *state* capitalism. The state insists on controlling its National Champions, for example, notwithstanding the fact that China too has ultimately privatized the bulk of its SOEs—albeit in a relatively gradual and controlled manner. The Soviet Union, in contrast, chose what is colloquially characterized as the Big Bang approach: a rapid and comprehensive privatization of publicly owned property in combination with instant price liberalization. Tragically, that approach resulted in a big bang indeed—namely, the nearly total collapse of the country's economy, as the overnight privatization of state-owned property turned into a giant orgy of looting of public assets by a handful of oligarchs.

This is not to suggest that China has simply avoided corruption and the plundering of public resources. When it comes to privatization, for example, management buyouts are notoriously susceptible to self-dealing, and numerous Chinese SOEs were sold to managers at grossly undervalued prices, giving rise to bitter protests. However, bribery under Chinese state capitalism takes distinctive forms. The most widespread form of corruption in China is not the outright theft of public

25 Ibid., 581.

assets but, rather, the provision of private *access* to them in exchange for favors, monetary or otherwise. For the political scientist Yuen Yuen Ang, this helps explain the coexistence of a booming economy with widespread venality: Selling access to resources *can* generate growth so long as that access goes to the highest bidder.[26] We might call this a kind of "political capitalism"—following Max Weber's characterization of the economy of the Roman empire—in which state-controlled resources are in effect auctioned at market prices.

Insofar as Chinese and post-Soviet capitalisms have taken divergent paths, this may also reflect differences in the socialisms that preceded them. The Stalinist version of a planned economy was a highly centralized one, seeking to realize a utopian ideal of bureaucratic omniscience. Its subsequent liberalization embraced an equally extreme and equally idealized view of self-regulating markets. As the economist Isabella Weber observes, substantively the two visions are radically opposed to one another, but they also share a certain fundamentalist faith in theoretical models' ability to deliver an optimal system.[27] Yet, tragically, the Soviet versions of socialism as well as capitalism collapsed in practice.

China, in contrast, has been more pragmatic in its embrace of both socialism *and* capitalism. As we have seen, Mao initially adopted the Soviet model of central planning, but as soon as some of its problems became apparent, he began to relax it, delegating more and more authority to lower levels. (To cite just one Chinese statistic, in the late 1970s only 791 types of products remained under direct planning by the central government, in contrast to the Soviet Union where that number reached 12 million.[28]) As to capitalism, the early Chinese reformers also

26 See Yuen Yuen Ang, *China's Gilded Age: The Paradox of Economic Boom and Vast Corruption* (Cambridge: Cambridge University Press, 2020).

27 Isabella Weber, *How China Escaped Shock Therapy: The Market Reform Debate* (Abingdon: Routledge, 2021), 262.

28 See James Kai-sing Kung, "From Industrialization to Urbanization: The Social Consequences of Changing Fiscal Incentives on Local Government

considered seriously the use of "shock therapy" in the form of wholesale price liberalization, yet they ultimately rejected that course and chose a more gradual approach instead.

Regardless of how we choose to characterize China's reforms and their outcomes, there is little question that today for the first time in China's history there exists an enormous class of impoverished and radically powerless industrial workers. It is an especially painful irony of history that there is no adequate vocabulary to describe or address their circumstances *because* of the very same reforms that have given rise to their current condition. As we saw in the chapter 2, in 1978 the Party announced that class struggle had been won, thus allowing the nation to turn its attention to economic development. In effect, it was the official retirement of "class" from the political lexicon that has made it possible for China's proletariat to emerge. With the restructuring of labor relations in SOEs, the formerly ideologically glorified—albeit politically subordinated—Chinese workers have been transformed into an army of servants of globalization.[29]

Looking back, then, it is clear that a once superordinated socialist working class has been transformed into a subordinated capitalist one. On the one hand, this loss of status has made it relatively more equal vis-à-vis the peasantry. On the other hand, after the state turned to global capital to invigorate its urban economy, the overall welfare gap between China's rural and urban economies has continued to widen even as the urban working class has continued to decline.

In the absence of a corresponding commodification of both land and labor in the countryside, the urban transformations outlined in this

---

Behavior," in David Kennedy and Joseph Stiglitz, eds., *Law and Economics with Chinese Characteristics* (Oxford: Oxford University Press, 2013), 493.

29 I borrow the term from Rhacel Salazar Parreñas, *Servants of Globalization: Women, Migration, and Domestic Work* (Stanford, CA: Stanford University Press, 2001). Parreñas uses the term specifically with reference to migrant Filipina domestic workers, but it is eminently applicable to proletarianized Chinese labor as well.

chapter represent only a partial transition to market society, to return to Karl Polanyi's characterization of the triumph of industrial capitalism. Let us turn next to the processes that have begun to absorb the peasant, too, into China's new proletariat. Paradoxically, the expropriation of the peasantry is the final—rather than first—step in this development, one that has critical consequences for the global economy and, indeed, the globe itself.

4

Unmaking the Peasant: Rural Proletarianization, 1994–Present

Not all historically significant violence takes the form of revolution.
—Barrington Moore Jr.,
Social Origins of Dictatorship and Democracy

We have seen how the revolution first made the socialist peasant, tying him to the land he owned through his collective. The post-1978 economic reforms gave rise to rural industry organized in the novel form of TVEs, which withered away when the state put the brakes on rural growth and turned to reforming its urban industries instead. In the 1990s, a new regime of state capitalism spelled the end of the iron rice bowl for industrial workers and inaugurated the full commodification of labor across the state sector and private industry—the unmaking of the Chinese working class—along with the commodification of urban land in the name of economic development. This industrial restructuring was accompanied by a growing tide of foreign capital that helped transform China's urban landscape. The rest, as we know, is history.

Yet it is emphatically not the end of history. To conclude the story here would indeed amount to a tale of capitalism's triumph, for better or for worse. It is now time to ask: Where do peasants and the countryside fit in China's urban transformation? Formally, nowhere. They have no official role to play and are expected to remain focused primarily on agriculture, with privatized TVEs playing a secondary role. This final chapter examines how the turn to urban development has nonetheless transformed the economic relationship between city and country as well as the way in which they are connected with each other through capitalist and socialist processes of accumulation.

When China's cities were hit by a tidal wave of foreign capital, they found themselves suddenly short on labor. The booming urban industry soon tapped into the vast reservoir of workers in the countryside, who have become a seemingly bottomless pool of migrant labor. In the process, what had been a transfer of resources from country to city under Maoism turned into a transfer of human beings. At first blush, this would seem to signal the closing of the era of primitive accumulation and a shift to wage labor and other ordinary forms of capitalist accumulation across urban and rural China. However, this chapter argues that the turn to migrant labor is best understood as Chinese state capitalism's continuing dependence on socialist institutions, most notably collective land ownership.

Even after the emergence of migrant labor, the conditions in the countryside itself remained at first unchanged, apart from the ebb and flow of villagers going to cities to work and then returning. Recently, however, marketization has reached even collectively held agricultural land, the last frontier in the commodification of humans' relationship to nature in China. To anticipate the conclusion of this chapter, remade peasants and unmade urban workers will become two streams flowing into a single river of proletarianized labor, overwhelming the geographic borders and class strictures that defined China's prereform economy. But first we must examine further the changing relationship between city and country. That will allow us to answer, finally, the question with which we began: Why dispossess the peasantry of its land when it has already been recruited to perform industrial labor at minimal wages?

We must begin by understanding the critical role played by the legacy of rural socialism in China's transformation into an economic superpower.

Rural Supply, Urban Demand

In the sociologist *cum* historian Giovanni Arrighi's formulation, the ultimate question for the PRC leadership has been "how to govern and develop a country with a rural population larger than the *entire* population of Africa, or Latin America, or Europe."[1] In economic terms, the Peasant Question is conventionally framed as that of "surplus agricultural labor" (*nongye shengyu laodongli*). In this view, there are simply too many peasants. With the emergence of TVEs in the early 1980s, a considerable portion of that surplus was absorbed by the new rural industry: By 1996, there were over 23 million rural enterprises employing some 135 million workers.[2]

Rural China's economic decline began with a restructuring of the fiscal system. Initially, the tax responsibility system established in 1980 had allowed rural governments to keep any "extrabudgetary" revenue they collected beyond the share they owed to the central government. It was precisely this arrangement that provided the economic motivation for townships and villages to establish enterprises whose profits they were able to retain and distribute locally. However, as we saw, in 1994 the deficit-ridden central government renewed its demand for a greater share of the rural surplus to help finance a new phase of predominantly urban reforms. This return to a more extractive fiscal relationship between city and country came to be known as the "peasant burden" (*nongmin fudan*), except now it fell to the peasant to support state capitalism rather than state socialism.

Rural industry in turn found itself caught between the state and the market. Cash-strapped local governments increased their fiscal demands on TVEs. At the same time, more and more rural credit was

1 Giovanni Arrighi, *Adam Smith in Beijing: Lineages of the Twenty-First Century* (London: Verso Books, 2007), 374 (emphasis in original).

2 Enrico C. Perotti, Laixiang Sun, and Liang Zou, "State-Owned Versus Township and Village Enterprises in China," *Comparative Economic Studies* 41, nos. 2–3 (1999): 152.

being directed to urban development, precisely at a time when TVEs were facing an economic downturn. By the late 1990s many had gone bankrupt or were privatized. No longer obligated to provide jobs to all households along with public goods, the privatized TVEs reduced their workforce. With the state prioritizing exports, rural industry—like its urban counterpart—became increasingly attuned to foreign markets. When the Asian financial crisis hit in 1997, TVEs faced further shutdowns and layoffs. To make matters worse, the agricultural sector too was subject to political and economic pressures. As the commodification of labor and land proceeded in cities, the state was keenly concerned with maintaining social order. Especially after breaking the SOE workers' iron rice bowl, it sought to maintain grain prices at an artificially low level—another way of making peasants subsidize urban workers. After accession to the WTO in 2001, agricultural imports inundated China's markets, contributing further to rural decline.

For urban industry, however, the WTO was a boon, opening the door even wider for global capital. With laid-off SOE workers looking for employment, the state had already began to welcome foreign direct investment (FDI) in the mid-1990s. By 2003, China had become the world's largest recipient of FDI, supplanting the United States. To help find markets for everything its workers produced, China also took several steps through the 1980s to devalue its currency, culminating in a one-time devaluation of the yuan by 33 percent in 1994—an event that marked a decisive turn to reliance on export-led growth. Just as China's chronic capital shortage was transformed into a capital glut, its trade deficits too soon turned into ever-increasing surpluses. The recently commodified urban land regime in turn became the literal foundation for the new era of state capitalism. Building office buildings and factories required massive amounts of labor, and once they were built, they too needed workers.

These were the economic conditions that led to the emergence of migrant labor: an endless surplus of labor in the countryside and an equally boundless urban demand for it. In some ways, this economic asymmetry was a return to the urban-rural imbalance that had structured China's economy since the 1950s but was temporarily reduced during the TVE boom in the 1980s. The *hukou* registration system had been put in place during agricultural collectivization precisely in order to achieve "industrialization without urbanization" and to prevent the rise of massive slums of the kind that had emerged first in England in the nineteenth century. Unlike its modernizing counterparts in Latin America, for example, China had succeeded—at a considerable human cost—in keeping its rural poor where they belonged: in the countryside. Accordingly, rural China had been burdened with a population surplus almost from the founding of the PRC.

But although the *hukou* registration system remained in place, in the 1990s China's rural workers finally found their way into cities en masse. Because of urban development and, specifically, the commodification of urban land, it became increasingly possible for peasants to defy their administrative status. The dismantling of urban work units had led to the emergence of new markets for housing, food, healthcare, and other essentials. So long as they could buy the necessities they needed, peasants were able to leave their villages, with or without an urban registration. They would remain second-class citizens in the city, to be sure, ineligible for subsidized housing, schooling for their children, and many other valuable urban benefits. Nonetheless, a life in the city—albeit a hard life—became not only conceivable but was often preferable to rural hardship.

To summarize, the initial reforms in the countryside had led to *rural industrialization* as a way out of poverty. The new urban reforms soon led to the eclipse of rural industry and gave rise to *rural migration* as a new economic strategy.

Contradictions of Migrant Labor

With the *hukou* registration system in place, rural newcomers' presence in the city is still temporary, at least legally. Accordingly, they end up in the most precarious parts of the economy, such as industrial factories and construction. When they lose their jobs (which happens regularly), do not get paid (not unusual), or suffer injuries at work (also not unusual), they move back to the villages where they are registered. For example, in the aftermath of the 2008 economic crisis, an estimated 25 million migrant workers lost their jobs and returned to their homes. Buffeted by fluctuating economic forces and their changing personal circumstances, they traverse continuously back and forth between city and country.

In sociological terms, a migrant worker is a hybrid. Legally speaking, he is a contradiction in terms. The colloquial term for migrant labor is *nongmin-gong*—literally, "peasant-worker." In the administrative logic of Chinese socialism, this is an oxymoron. A "peasant" in the proper sense is engaged in tilling the land, while a "worker" toils in urban industry. There is no coherent legal or structural position for a person who is both. Although migrant workers most certainly work, their labor lacks the dignity of that of socialist workers. The colloquial term used to characterize migrant laborers' activity—*dagong*—connotes alienated labor performed for someone other than oneself. The gendered vernacular designations *dagong zai* and *dagong mei* can in turn be translated as "working boy" and "working girl," suggesting these workers' relative youth as well as the casualized nature of their labor.

Especially young women often envision a stint in a textile or electronics factory as a temporary opportunity to make money before returning to the village to marry and to care for parents and in-laws. One side effect of the decollectivization of agriculture has been a revival of traditional gender norms in the countryside. As we have seen, during the Maoist era women participated in both agricultural work and public projects and were compensated for their labor, thus raising their economic and social status. The establishment of markets may signify modernization but they have also paved the way for the reemergence of "feudal superstition" and a host of practices that had been more or less eliminated, such as the rise of popular religion, payment of bride price upon marriage, and prostitution. Indeed, the ideology of radical sameness associated with state socialism—exemplified most visibly by both men and women donning Mao jackets—created its own backlash in the 1980s, with a return to the celebration of femininity and gender difference. After the decollectivization of agriculture rural women have returned largely to their traditional domestic roles. Many young women in particular have come to view the city as a site of adventure and potential freedom—dreams that are not necessarily fulfilled but reflect the confined nature of their rural existence.

Collectively, migrant laborers form the core of a larger population of irregular denizens in the city. Marked by their lack of a permanent urban registration, they are shut out of numerous services as well as social respectability. Their uncertain status is reflected in the vernacular term used to characterize them: "floating population" (*liudong renkou*). In a system that prizes fixity, to refuse one's assigned spatial coordinates is inherently subversive, as we observed in chapter 1. While all states are threatened by mobile subjects, in China the fear of unattached citizens is especially potent, owing both to the historic threat posed by nomadic peoples just beyond its borders and the fact that the Chinese state established a population registry far earlier than European states did—the ancestor of the *hukou*, originally set up for tax collection.[3]

Reflecting this history, the late imperial state was especially concerned about roving men with no discernible attachments, personified by propertyless unmarried rural youth with neither land nor family to tie them down. In the legal terminology of the Qing Code, these surplus males were known as *guanggun*, or "rootless rascals."[4] In a similar manner,

3 For an astute historical analysis of the *hukou* system, see Michael R. Dutton, *Policing and Punishment in China: From Patriarchy to "the People"* (Cambridge: Cambridge University Press, 1992), 189–245.

4 This is Matthew Sommer's felicitous translation of the term *guanggun*, usually translated literally as "bare sticks." Although "bare sticks" is less meaningful in English than "rootless rascals," it too suggests the alienation of the young men to whom the term refers: Sticks are by definition not attached to a larger (family) tree and are thus literally rootless. See Matthew H. Sommer,

the PRC's first criminal law, enacted in 1979, addressed most petty crime by penalizing an offense commonly translated as "hooliganism" (*liumangzui*). It is no accident, then, that *liudong renkou* resonates with the Chinese term for "hooligan," *liumang*, which indeed combines the association of lack of fixity with criminality.

These social distinctions continue to inform the public's evaluation of the floating population today, associated with the rise of a rhetoric of *suzhi*, referring to a person's "quality." This discourse forms part of an anti-rural ideology that associates the countryside with people of "low quality" and the urban milieu with citizens of "high quality." This is in effect a new class discourse, one that indexes social rather than political class. In the Maoist taxonomy, the peasant was suspect because he represented an antiquated mode of production. *Suzhi*, while notoriously ineffable, denotes a person's character and subjective developmental attributes rather than his or her objective economic circumstances. At its most extreme, it renders the rural-urban distinction a quasi-ethnic one, as if the city and the country were inhabited by two different kinds of human beings. In this vision a peasant-worker is something like a centaur: half human, half less-than-human.

Despite the state's preference for stationary subjects, moving back and forth between city and country is far from a new phenomenon. As we saw in chapter 1, in the late imperial era the boundary was fluid, and it is the PRC's efforts to segregate the city from the country that constitutes a radical departure from tradition. The practice of sojourning—maintaining an attachment to one's native place while establishing a long-term residency elsewhere—was widespread in the Ming and the Qing. Absentee landlords dwelt in the city while preserving an economic, social, and psychological investment in the country, mediated through Confucian ancestral institutions. Successful urban entrepreneurs in turn preferred to plow their profits into rural land. By joining the gentry, they sought to convert their economic wealth into social capital, and like their rural counterparts—the

---

Sex, Law, and Society in Late Imperial China (Stanford, CA: Stanford University Press, 2000), 10 and throughout.

absentee landlords traveling in the opposite direction—they too moved between two worlds. These traditions of sojourning came to provide a basis for international labor migrations as well, first to Southeast Asia and then to Europe and the Americas as well. Challenging a binary distinction between merely temporary residence overseas and permanent emigration, many if not most diasporic Chinese envisioned themselves ultimately returning home—at least spiritually if not physically—even as they invested in new futures in new places. Today's migrant worker finds himself in a similar predicament, albeit within China: both aspiring to belong while yearning to return.[5]

Yet, as we have noted, the imperial state's attitude to its subjects' mobility was inflected by class. Geographically unattached landlords did not threaten existing social hierarchies, in contrast to the peripatetic poor, epitomized by "rootless rascals." Like its imperial predecessor, the PRC is especially anxious about the uncontrolled mobility of unmarried and unpropertied young men. While all migrant workers are considered a general threat to social order, the male ones are seen as sexually dangerous as well. One of the gendered consequences of the one-child policy instituted in the reform era has been the resurgence of a male-female imbalance. As a result, many rural men *cannot* marry even if they wish to. Especially when they become part of the floating population, they are viewed as a potential sexual threat to decent women or, even worse, they may choose to become "Money Boys"—that is, young men who make a living by selling sexual services mostly, though not necessarily exclusively, to men.

5 Numerous aspects of the porous traditional boundary between city and country are explored in William Skinner's classic volume, *The City in Late Imperial China* (Stanford, CA: Stanford University Press, 1977). Important studies of the transnational mobility of Chinese labor include Madeline Hsu, *Dreaming of Gold, Dreaming of Home: Transnationalism and Migration Between the United States and South China, 1882–1943* (Stanford, CA: Stanford University Press, 2000), and Mae Ngai, *The Chinese Question: The Gold Rushes and Global Politics* (New York: W. W. Norton, 2021).

With migrant labor there has emerged also a new class of entrepreneurs to bridge the gap between city and country. Labor brokers are arbitrageurs who help transform peasants' labor power into a commodity. Most peasants live in relative geographic, social, and administrative isolation. Wen Tiejun refers to the countryside as China's "internal Third World" (*neibu de disan shijie*), highlighting the unequal structural relationship between city and country.[6] By arranging the logistics of transportation and financing, labor brokers link peasants to the production chains of global capital.

To the extent that middlemen are quintessential colonial actors—once known as "comprador capitalists" in the argot of Chinese socialism—these rural labor brokers are in some ways contemporary counterparts of the intermediaries who facilitated the international exportation of Chinese coolie labor in the era of semicolonialism. In the nineteenth century, it fell to Asian labor to go to where Euro-American capital was located. At that moment, labor was needed above all for infrastructure and extractive projects such as railroads and mining in the American West, Australia, and South Africa, most notably—undertakings that were geographically fixed. In contrast, in the current age of globalization industrial capital is mobile and goes wherever cheap labor is located. What has not changed is that just as coolie labor in the nineteenth century ranged from coerced to voluntary, so too with rural migrants. Often, "labor broker" is a euphemism for a labor trafficker.

Remarkably, however, the migration of hundreds of millions of people has not resulted in the erection of massive slums—an outcome the PRC has tirelessly sought to avoid. There has been unrest, to be sure,

---

6 Wen Tiejun, "Shichanghua yu Xiaonong Jingji [Marketization and the Small Peasant Economy]," in Wen Tiejun, *Jiegou Xiandaihua: Wen Tiejun Yanjiang Lu* [Deconstructing Modernization: Lectures by Wen Tiejun] (Guangzhou: Guangdong Renmin Chubanshe, 2004), 103. For elaboration on this analogy by Wen and others, see Alexander F. Day, *The Peasant in Postsocialist China: History, Politics, and Capitalism* (Cambridge: Cambridge University Press, 2013), 126.

but the state has been extraordinarily successful in localizing and containing it. In order to understand why, let us turn to the organization of migrant labor.

Communist Foundations of Chinese Capitalism

The socialist compounds of SOEs are gone, but the new labor regime that has replaced them is no less totalizing in its scope, albeit without the leavening effects of socialist paternalism. While the classic SOE was a factory *cum* miniature welfare state, migrant laborers who work for megacorporations are warehoused in enormous dormitories that are essentially corporate labor camps. In global media, these high-security facilities with military-style labor discipline are exemplified by Foxconn, the infamous multinational electronics manufacturer. Its facilities in Shenzhen, known as the "Forbidden City," include dozens of dormitories, shops, and a hospital, with public order maintained by over 1,000 security officers. Notoriously, the company's CEO referred to his employees in 2011 as "one million animals," although he later clarified that he did not intend his words as an insult.[7] (Like Adam Smith, he apparently does not distinguish between human and animal labor.) These labor camps may well be dystopian and inhumane, but they are the very opposite of chaotic shanty towns endangering public order, as the workers are more likely to kill themselves than their bosses.

It is a commonplace in the discourse of globalization that China's "comparative advantage" is its cheap labor. As the political scientist Lin Chun notes, it is dubious to call it an advantage when a nation's relative poverty obligates it to sell its labor to foreign buyers at bargain rates.[8]

7 Henry Blodget, "Foxconn: Yes, Our CEO Called Our Employees 'Animals' But He Didn't Mean It as an Insult," *Business Insider*, January 20, 2012, businessinsider.com.

8 Lin Chun, *The Transformation of Chinese Socialism* (Durham, NC: Duke University Press, 2006), 286.

What is more, there are numerous countries far poorer than China that are able to provide far cheaper labor, yet they do not hold the same appeal for global capital. China's real advantage is at least threefold: the high quality of its workforce, its superior infrastructure, and its sociopolitical stability. With respect to the quality of Chinese workers, they are valued highly (albeit compensated poorly) because they are healthy, educated, and disciplined.

These attributes are a direct legacy of Chinese socialism. As we have seen, the first decades after the establishment of the PRC witnessed significant increases in literacy and health, especially in the countryside. While free-market ideologues routinely ascribe China's post-1978 economic success to its emancipation from the shackles of communism, one of the most critical factors in its rise has been the superior quality of its socialist-trained workforce. Even the military-style work discipline in today's factories owes a great deal to the Cultural Revolution, as attested by managers who greet their employees by shouting "How are you?" and drill them to respond in unison, "Good! Very good! Very, very good!"[9] For better or worse, Chinese capitalism is deeply indebted to its socialist past.

But it is not only socialism's past but also its lingering presence in rural China that continues to subsidize the urban economy. That subsidy is built into the labor migration regime itself, and it is the ultimate contributor to the "cheapness" of China's workers. The market for migrant workers has allowed capital—including Chinese private and state capital as well as global investors—to transform China's rural population into what Marx called a reserve army of labor, or a surplus population that bears the costs of its own reproduction. Lacking access to urban benefits, the provision of migrant workers' welfare falls to their families as they shuttle back and forth between factories and villages. Peasant-workers' entitlement to land at home is effectively their social security.

9 Pun Ngai, *Migrant Labor in China: Post-Socialist Transformations* (Malden, MA: Polity Press, 2016), 122.

To be sure, historically cities everywhere have relied on the countryside to restock their populations. Before modern sanitation systems—long before the emergence of capitalism—urban mortality rates were so high that cities could not reproduce their citizenry without replenishing it with a continual stream of healthier arrivals from the country. This became even more so under the lethal conditions of early industrial capitalism. Today China's villagers help support not only the existing migrant laborers but also bear the costs of their literal reproduction by giving birth to and raising new generations of workers, while also shouldering the costs of caring for superannuated workers once their productive capacity has been depleted. It is precisely the remains of rural socialism—above all uncommodified agricultural land—that subsidizes China's urban capitalism. But for this land regime, migrant workers would not be able to toil at such low wages.

It is vital to recognize that the exploitation of rural labor is emphatically not unique to China nor is it evidence of an especially cruel form of Asian capitalism. Reliance on various kinds of migrant laborers—"legal" as well as "undocumented"—who are paid cut-rate wages is one of the main ways in which primitive accumulation proceeds today around the world, whether under socialism or capitalism. All of the major popular revolutions of the twentieth century took place in agrarian societies and were fought by peasants. Short of subordinating themselves to foreign capital, these new revolutionary states—like all preindustrial economies, starting with England—had no choice but to rely on some form of domestic primitive accumulation for their modernization, and the main burden of their development was borne by the peasantry.

While there may be nothing especially distinctive about peasants migrating to cities and turning into an urban proletariat, what *is* distinctive about China is that its peasant-workers have not been fully urbanized. Rather, they have become a *migrant* labor force, one that remains in a perpetual state of dislocation, journeying back and forth between city and country. One of the few comparable examples is South Africa. To obtain cheap labor for its mines and cities, it too relied systematically on a regime of legally enforced geographic segregation. Not unlike the *hukou* system, the apartheid regime prevented black workers from taking up permanent residence in cities, forcing them instead to divide themselves between townships and cities.

In effect, the Chinese migrant worker represents an unequal combination of two modes of production, marking an incomplete shift from primitive socialist accumulation to ordinary modes of capitalist accumulation. Under socialism, the state requisitioned the *product* of peasants' labor—a classic instance of primitive socialist accumulation. Today, urban capital extracts the healthiest and most productive *peasants themselves* for its use, albeit only on a temporary basis. On the one hand, migrant workers earn their living by performing wage labor, thus incorporating themselves into the institutions of urban state capitalism. On the other hand, insofar as they continue to depend on their villages as well for support, they remain tethered to the enduring core feature of rural socialism, namely, collectively owned land. It is these rural ties that stall migrant peasants' full transition to a capitalist labor force.

To summarize, the unmaking of the privileged urban working class consisted in the state's disavowal of its obligations to its industrial workforce. After the breaking of the iron rice bowl, they became an ordinary working class in the capitalist sense. But even after abnegating its responsibilities to urban workers, the state has continued to draw resources from the country. Practices of primitive socialist accumulation have not ceased—they have only taken reconfigured forms. The crucial difference consists in *who benefits* from uncompensated peasant labor. Under state socialism, the rural subsidy accrued primarily to urban industrial workers. Today, its chief beneficiary is urban capital. The rural land regime is the key to China's "cheap labor" and thus the ultimate secret of China's global success. Together, the unmade working class and the remade peasantry have paved the way for the rise of a new economic superpower—an improbable merger of capitalism and socialism.

It is indeed important to emphasize that the rise of Chinese migrant labor constitutes an essential structural element of *global* capitalism and thus part of *our* economic regime as well. In the first place, it has corresponded to a simultaneous deindustrialization of the US economy. To the extent that North Atlantic capital has migrated to China in quest of cheap labor, it has led to the disappearance of manufacturing jobs in the United States. Effectively, the unmaking of the Chinese working class has coincided with the unmaking of the American working class. At the same time, the substitution of Chinese imports for domestic manufactures has driven up America's trade deficit. For China hawks and conservative policy analysts this is evidence that China is taking advantage of the United States, as they recall nostalgically the era after World War II when goods "made in the USA" were the envy of the world and the nation enjoyed a seemingly permanent trade surplus.

Yet it is not so simple to determine who is taking advantage of whom. So long as the United States' postwar economic supremacy was reflected in trade surpluses, the benefits of that supremacy accrued to capital *and* labor. Those benefits were assuredly not divided evenly, but in the golden era of American manufacturing capital enjoyed healthy corporate profits while industrial workers were also paid a living wage. In contrast, the subsequent economic globalization has been ruinous for the working class. With the exodus of capital to China and other low-wage destinations, decent manufacturing jobs have all but disappeared. Capital, in contrast, is enjoying an unprecedented Gilded Age, transforming "cheap labor" from around the world into record profits for multinational corporations, which are in turn reflected in endlessly rising stock prices.

What is more, every American consumer is also a beneficiary of the Chinese migrant worker's "cheap labor." Indeed, as we have seen it is not just the overworked but able-bodied Chinese worker who makes it possible for us to buy as much as we do at bargain prices; it is also these workers' aged and less able relatives in far-flung rural villages that subsidize our metropolitan lives. The ultimate key to China's soi-disant cheap labor is the *free labor* performed by the rural kin who support outgoing migrants, making China's countryside the world's countryside, too. As George Orwell said in 1939, "What we always forget is that the overwhelming bulk of the British proletariat does not live in Britain but in

Asia and Africa."[10] The Chinese industrial workforce today, too, is a global proletariat, supporting consumers around the world.

Meanwhile Chinese workers' precarity constrains them to consume minimally and to save maximally. Their sense of insecurity is one of the chief causes of China's astonishing savings rate, which makes it possible for China to continue to buy seemingly unlimited amounts of US Treasuries. This helps keep interest rates low in the United States and pay for America's budget deficits, allowing both the US government and American consumers to live beyond their means. From this perspective, the US trade deficit with China looks much more like a free lunch than the Chinese proletariat taking advantage of Americans. To be sure, this lunch isn't literally free: The United States does have to pay for the goods it imports. But unlike other countries, it is able to do so simply by printing money. So long as the dollar remains the global reserve currency, the United States has the unique ability to finance its trade imbalance by issuing more Treasuries and relying on cheap credit, unlike a "normal" government.

Returning to the historical comparison with England, the contrast is instructive. England's trade deficit with China reached world-historic proportions in the eighteenth and nineteenth centuries, with British imports of tea and other Chinese goods skyrocketing, while Chinese buyers had little interest in British manufactures. Since China demanded

---

10 See Douglas Kerr, *Orwell and Empire* (Oxford: Oxford University Press, 2022), 71. Significantly, the exploitation of rural China for "cheap labor" has a much a longer pedigree. In the so-called Treaty Ports dominated by Western powers in the late nineteenth and early twentieth centuries, Western capital depended on labor-rich peasant households for the production of cheap raw materials. As the historian Philip Huang observes, the most successful Western industries in the Shanghai-dominated Yangzi Delta in the late nineteenth century were those that were able to take advantage of the peasant economy for the most labor-intensive parts of their production, such as foreign silk producers who relied on rural sericulture. Philip C. C. Huang, *The Peasant Family and Rural Development in the Yangzi Delta, 1350–1988* (Stanford, CA: Stanford University Press, 1990).

to be paid in silver—it would not have dreamt of accepting notes from the Bank of England—English merchants had no choice but to find bullion or something they could actually sell. Notoriously, the East India Company solved the problem by resorting to opium, leading to the First Opium War (1839–42), which finally forced the Chinese to allow the importation of this noxious merchandise under the guise of "free trade." Fortunately for Americans, global trade is no longer conducted in silver, and ever since the United States abandoned the gold standard in 1971, its ability to print money has not been limited by its supply of precious metals either. Yanis Varoufakis, the former minister of finance of Greece, calls America's ability to finance its endless deficits simply by printing more money "a magic trick for the ages," characterizing the US trade imbalance as a form of "economic tribute" flowing from China to America.[11]

Let us return from the global perspective to that of the Chinese domestic economy. While rural and urban China remain far apart, with the rise of migrant labor an earlier state-enforced status inequality between peasants and socialist workers is increasingly overwhelmed by a simple distinction between the rich and the poor. Paradoxically, the emergence of a genuinely national labor market has resulted in a new kind of equality. Although rural migrants cannot aspire to the dignity of a classic SOE worker, after the contractualization of *all* labor state workers are no longer guaranteed a share of the benefits of economic development either. Together, the approximately 100 million laid-off state workers and more than 295 million migrant workers are increasingly merging in a single race to the bottom.[12]

Stated differently, the growing equality between rural and urban labor has been achieved by leveling down the status of the urban worker,

---

11 Yanis Varoufakis, *Technofeudalism: What Killed Capitalism?* (Brooklyn: Melville House, 2024), 449.

12 Pun Ngai estimates the number of laid-off state workers at 100 million. Ngai, *Migrant Labor in China*, 2. According to official Chinese statistics, the total number of migrant workers stood at 295.62 million at the end of 2022; https://www.stats.gov.cn/english/PressRelease/202302/t20230227_1918979.html.

rather than leveling up that of the migrant worker. Moreover, as noted above, former SOE employees have lost not only their economic security but also the ideological prestige they once enjoyed, as they too are increasingly viewed as persons of "low quality," akin to their migrant counterparts. Indeed, their social devaluation notwithstanding, migrant workers are increasingly viewed as even *superior* to the extent that they expect less from their employers as well as the state. Unlike urbanites, they are "flexible" and "self-reliant," and while they may be poor, they are nonetheless credited with having made China's economic miracle possible. In effect, the former state worker has come to be seen as a socio-economic problem and the migrant worker as its solution.

It is no small irony that migrant peasants are being incorporated into China's urban working class precisely at the moment when membership in that class has been devalued. Yet despite their publicly acknowledged economic importance they have even greater difficulty than former state workers in finding an effective and politically intelligible language to protest their conditions. Laid-off SOE employees were able to invoke the welfare guarantees they had enjoyed under socialism. Migrant laborers cannot claim to have lost a privileged status they never had, nor do they have a similar institutional basis for organizing collectively. A socialist work unit was, by definition, a community—albeit one under the discipline of the Party—and when work units were disbanded, their members were already united by bonds of solidarity. The units' cellular nature made it difficult to assemble coalitions beyond a single workplace, but at least they provided a basic building block for staging resistance and protest. Migrant workers, in contrast, are by definition transient employees who find themselves in alien environments, often crammed into corporate labor camps under intensive technologies of surveillance.

Migrant workers have thus been more likely than redundant state workers to resort to law when fired illegally or injured on the job, turning to individual dispute resolution in lieu of collective protest. This is often even less effective than staging a protest. Although Chinese employment law today contains numerous protections, its enforcement is left to local authorities, who are frequently more concerned with local economic development than the rights of workers hailing from elsewhere. Moreover, the legal system is by definition reactive. It cannot address a claim until one is brought, and it is the workers' own responsibility to defend their rights, even in conditions where they lack the social and economic resources to do so. Many workers do not even have employment contracts, although they have been mandatory since 1994. Strikingly, it is the peasants who have stayed in the countryside that have been more likely to protest their circumstances. Unlike their migrant kinfolk, they remain embedded in village communities which have continued to provide at least a rudimentary basis for collective action even after the abolition of collective farming.

A New Enclosure Movement

Ever since the arrival of global capital captured the state's, and the world's, imagination, rural China was largely sidelined from political and intellectual debates. However, by the turn of the millennium the cumulative effects of the neglect of rural institutions were fully in evidence, and the Party became again aware of peasants' revolutionary potential. Not only were villages deteriorating economically and hollowing out socially, but the financial health of local governments continued to decline as well because of the fiscal restructuring enacted as part of the state's turn to urban development in 1994. That restructuring, as we saw, increased local governments' tax burden, further compromising their ability to deliver services. Indeed, agricultural taxes—the detested "peasant burden"—were one of the main causes of rural unrest, until they were surpassed by an even more explosive concern: peasants' losing land.

Let us return again to the English comparison. In China, as in England, peasants have constituted a reserve army of labor for the development of industrial capital. However, unlike in England, in China the commodification of labor took place in industrial workplaces *before* a large-scale expropriation of rural land. We have already seen that the establishment of rural industry in the form of TVEs did not call for the expropriation of the peasants because TVEs were structured as collectives. Subsequently, it was the peasants' continued entitlement to rural land that also made it possible for them to become a *migrant* labor force, rooted in the countryside and semi-reliant on it. Why, then, dispossess a peasantry that has already submitted to capital voluntarily, or in Marx's formulation, under "the silent compulsion of economic relations"?[13]

This returns us to the hybridity of the migrant worker's condition, marking a partial shift from a regime of primitive socialist accumulation to primitive capitalist accumulation. Although both regimes are exploitative, the peasant's status differs under each. Under Maoism, the countryside was kept poor deliberately as it was harnessed to subsidize the urban state sector. Nonetheless the state attended to the health and literacy of its rural population—a healthy peasant is a productive peasant after all. In contrast, state capitalism is more concerned with short-term profit than the long-term health of its human capital. The migrant labor regime not only taxes the health and well-being of the workers themselves, but it also compounds the material and psychological stress of those who remain behind. Today, the despoliation of rural China for its human and natural resources is running against its limits.

Recognizing the mounting rural crisis, in the early 2000s the PRC began to enact health and retirement programs that would extend its new, predominantly urban social security institutions to the countryside. However, many of the new welfare mandates have been unfunded, placing new burdens on already distressed local governments. Many of these programs are also mandatory only down to the level of township governments, with villages free to opt out. Since local governments' human capital is increasingly damaged and depleted, many are turning to their only remaining asset: land. The process whereby rural jurisdictions have converted their collectively owned farmland into a freely alienable commodity is part of a larger phenomenon known as "land finance" (*tudi caizheng*), or the use of revenue from land sales to make

13 Karl Marx, *Capital*, vol. 1 (New York: Vintage Books, 1977), 899.

up local deficits. Between 2000 and 2017, more than half of local governments' fiscal revenue came from land finance.[14]

Let us turn, then, from investigating the commodification of rural labor to the commodification of rural land—that is, the so-called New Enclosure Movement. As noted in the introduction, it has resulted in land takings on a scale that is "unprecedented in human history," giving rise to a rapidly expanding population known as "land-losing peasants" (*shidi nongmin*).[15] It is also important to acknowledge, again, that officially *all* land in China remains publicly owned. This is an ideological necessity. The notion that "the People" own the land on which the People's Republic stands is the moral as well as legal ground of the Party's sovereignty. Hence, neither urban nor rural land can be sold outright. As in cities, so in the countryside, too, legally it is only the right to *use* land that has been commodified, rather than ownership in land "itself."

Until recently, collectively owned rural land could be used only for agriculture and for industrial purposes that support agriculture. As we have seen, those use rights could not be transferred beyond the membership of the collective. Stated differently, in the absence of a market, land cultivated by a rural household had only a use value, and no exchange value. But because rural land is owned by the collective, in contrast to state-owned urban land, its commodification has posed not only ideological but also far more challenging legal and administrative problems. Structurally the commodification of urban land was relatively simple. The state proceeded to alienate use rights to land it already owned. To be sure, this gave rise to protests, but the obstacles were essentially political in nature. The commodification of rural land, in contrast, is more complicated both politically and technically. Ideologically, it is even more controversial for the state to commodify land owned by peasants,

14 Xu Nannan, "What Gave Rise to China's Land Finance?," *Land Use Policy* 87, no. 1 (1999).

15 Chun Peng, *Rural Land Takings Law in Modern China: Origin and Revolution* (Cambridge: Cambridge University Press, 2018), 3.

in contrast to urban land it already owns in its own name. Moreover, because rural land could be used legally only for agriculture and associated purposes, in order to be able to sell it to commercial developers the state would have to reclassify it first as urban.

While this approach solved one problem, it created others. Under the hierarchical administrative logic of the PRC, a village cannot reclassify its lands as urban on its own: An adjacent municipality has to requisition the village land first. This is the point at which what might be a simple commodification of an existing right to use land turns into an expropriation. Once land is reclassified as urban, it is the *city* which owns the right to use it and has the authority to sell it to private developers. Legally, the villagers must be compensated for the loss of their land, but what makes this a de facto expropriation is the legally defined standard for compensation.

That standard is based on the land's value in its agricultural use, which is only a fraction of its post-conversion value as urban land. Indeed it is precisely that difference that motivates the conversion in the first place. To be sure, law also requires that any taking of land—urban or rural—must be in the public interest, but so long as the proceeds help make up for a budgetary shortfall, presumably almost any taking will meet that standard.[16] Moreover, both the manner in which the villagers' compensation is paid and the way in which the proceeds are spent can be subject to further irregularities. Even the less-than-adequate official compensation may not reach the villagers when corrupt village officials are involved, and even when it does, it is far from enough for being able to afford to live in the cities in which they suddenly find themselves—without jobs, land, or social security. Essentially, the villagers become rural migrants not because they have moved but because the rural-urban boundary has.

16 Zhonghua Renmin Gongheguo Tudi Guanli Fa [Land Administration Law of the People's Republic of China] (promulgated by the Standing Committee of the National People's Congress June 25, 1986, most recently amended Aug. 26, 2019), article 2.

In practice, the processes of land-taking vary considerably from village to village, reflecting differences in regional development, a village's proximity to a city, and the integrity of local officials. With development, the potential market value of peri-urban land has skyrocketed, and villages abutting an urban border are often already semi-industrialized, legally or not. Some villages in the wealthy Pearl River Delta with savvy leadership and a history of rural industry have even turned themselves into the legal form of a corporation, managing to negotiate for "reserve land" which they develop commercially in their own account, effectively transforming themselves from farmers to rentier capitalists (*shouzu jieji*).[17] In contrast to such entrepreneurial villages *cum* corporations, poor peasants in less developed areas are likely to be dispossessed for little compensation.

Even ostensibly voluntary development is frequently riddled with corruption. What happened in the village of Wukan in Eastern Guangdong in 2011 represents a typical scenario. Local officials arranged with a real estate company to convert village land for development. While purporting to represent the village, however, the officials did so without the villagers' agreement, pocketing the money for themselves. This strategy is essentially a contemporary variant of colonial practices of dispossession in the New World and elsewhere, with settlers' paying off tribal leaders to sign formal sale documents without tribe members' consent. Indeed, similar legal chicanery was an integral part of the original Enclosure Movement in England as well, especially in its early stages.

With China's real estate boom, it is not surprising that many villagers have not been content to wait to be expropriated by urban governments, private developers, and corrupt village officials. Instead, they have developed their land themselves, typically by building housing either for sale or rent, often to migrant laborers working in nearby cities who cannot afford legally approved housing. The fact that such development

17 See, for example, You-tien Hsing, *The Great Urban Transformation: Politics of Land and Property in China* (Oxford: Oxford University Press, 2010)

is technically illegal has not stopped it. A vast market in unauthorized real estate, known as "small property" (*xiaochanquan*) exists in contrast to legal, and therefore more expensive, "big property" (*dachanquan*). We can think of the development of small property as a kind of "self-enclosure" of collectively owned village land—taking the land, and the law, into one's own hands.[18]

Small property may also be considered a kind of protest against the state's developmental policies. Others, however, have resorted to more direct ways of registering their discontent, and rural tax protests have been superseded by protests against the expropriation of land. Like their urban counterparts, they can take many forms from setting up roadblocks to refusing to leave the land, with the number of participants varying from a single household to mass protests involving hundreds, and even thousands, as in the case of the violent confrontations in Wukan in 2011, which garnered national and international attention.

Capitalism Arrives in the Countryside

In the early 2000s, the state finally began to take steps to address a rural crisis of its own making. Each year the State Council issues a so-called No. 1 Document to outline its major policies. In 2004 the No. 1 Document focused on agriculture, for the first time since 1986. In 2005, the state embarked on a campaign to build a New Socialist Countryside (*shehui zhuyi xin nongcun*), with subsidies for rural infrastructure projects. In 2006, it finally abolished the detested Agricultural Tax. These steps represented a major volte-face in the economic relationship between city and country: Instead of extracting resources from the countryside, the state began to direct them back to villages. In the official rhetoric of the Party, it was time for "industry to help agriculture" (*gongye fanbu nongye*) rather than vice versa.

18 Qiao Shitong, *Chinese Small Property: The Co-Evolution of Law and Social Norms* (Cambridge: Cambridge University Press, 2017).

In fact, this was not just rhetoric. When the Global Financial Crisis hit in 2008, migrant workers were the main shock absorber as always, returning to their villages after being laid off. The government responded the same way it had responded to the Asian financial crisis in 1997–1998, namely, with massive state investments in infrastructure. However, this time a significant portion of the public expenditure was directed to the countryside, including spending on rural health, education, and environmental projects.

One key objective of the campaign for building a New Socialist Countryside was to put the brakes on urban expansion into surrounding countryside. The goal now was to urbanize the countryside without displacing the villagers (*litu bulixiang*, or "leave the soil without leaving the countryside"), for example, by bringing apartment-style housing to villages and thus vacating land for commercial development. Yet the new projects did not quell peasant dissatisfaction, as the bulk of government support went to developers rather than peasants. In 2014, the state reversed direction, setting out a New Style Urbanization Plan (*xinxing chengzhenhua guihua*). Instead of urbanizing peasants while keeping them in place, the aim was now to relocate villagers into cities, with the ultimate goal of converting 100 million rural *hukou* holders into urban citizens.

Even as the state has turned to urbanization and real estate development as alternative methods of stimulating economic growth, it also recognizes that China's leading cities cannot absorb more migrants, at least not without the prospect of slums rising on urban outskirts. It is therefore directing the flow of rural migration to small and medium-sized cities as well as so-called New Cities (*xincheng*)—brand-new housing developments, often hastily built and associated with poor infrastructure and substandard services.

The state promotes a paternalistic discourse about "letting peasants upstairs" (*rang nongmin shanglou*) and allowing them "to exchange land for social welfare" (*tudi huan shebao*), but such slogans mean little when there is no welfare and there are no viable urban jobs, especially for the older and less educated arrivals. As one recently urbanized peasant observed, "Even though we have the paper that says we are urban, it seems we are actually not."[19] Today, many peasants with a rural *hukou* would prefer to stay in their villages and maintain their entitlement to land. Ironically, for decades the household registration system was a means of coercing peasants to stay in the countryside, but now that the value of rural land has increased and the value of an urban registration has decreased, the *hukou* system is being used for coercive urbanization.

The New Style Urbanization policy coincided with the launching of a so-called New Land Reform (*xin tudi zhidu gaige*), aiming to consolidate farmland so as to promote more efficient and modern cultivation. Since 2008, the state has expressed its preference for what is sometimes referred to as the consolidation, chemicalization, commercialization, and mechanization (CCCM) of agriculture.[20] Especially in densely populated areas, household-based plots are often too small to support mechanized commercial farming. In order to scale up China's agriculture, the state wants to create vertically integrated production chains that link cultivators with the processing and marketing of what they produce.

Viewed together, New Style Urbanization and New Land Reform are two sides of the same coin. While the former addresses the Peasant Question—by seeking to transform peasants into urbanites—the latter takes on the Land Question. The New Land Reform itself is in effect a polite euphemism for *reversing* the original one in 1950, which distributed land from rich landowners to peasants. In contrast, the current one seeks to consolidate peasants' small household plots into large industrial farms operated by agribusiness. Together with the policy of "letting capital go to the countryside" (*rang ziben dao nongcun qu*), the goal is to create ever greater concentrations of both capital and land.

19 Julia Chuang and John Yasuda, "Polanyi and the Peasant Question in China: State, Peasant, and Land Relations in China, 1949–Present," *Politics and Society* 50, no. 2 (2022): 331.

20 Stevan Harrell, *An Ecological History of Modern China* (Seattle: University of Washington Press, 2023), 246.

Typically, all dispossessed peasants are categorized as "land-losing peasants." However, it is important to recognize the qualitatively different nature of the more recent wave of enclosures. As we saw, the first one essentially enlarged urban China's footprint by incorporating adjacent villages. It did not commodify rural land as such but simply reclassified it legally as urban land. In contrast, the current phase is aimed at the heart of rural China itself. To aggregate the collectively owned but individually cultivated household plots that have defined China's countryside since the establishment of the Household Responsibility System, even rural land is being finally commodified qua rural land.

As in the case of urban land, formally it is only the right to the land's use—rather than the land "itself"—that is being commodified. From its inception the Household Responsibility System too distinguished between ownership (by collective) and use (by individual households), but that use was not alienable. To be sure, some households leased their plots to other households anyway, but they did so without legal authorization. When the Land Administration Law was revised in 1998, the practice was legalized but transfers remained subject to collective approval and limited to agricultural use only. The law was revised again in 2019 and together with the Rural Contract Law, revised in 2018, it finally made it possible to transfer one's use rights to non-villagers and other market actors, with the official caveat that any transfer must not diminish the overall amount of arable land.[21] In absolute terms, the state

21 In Xiaoqian Hu's formulation, the revised Land Administration Law "essentially . . . abolished the decades old dualist land system." "Put That Bucket Down! Money, Politics, and Property Rights in Urbanizing China," *Vermont Law Review* 44, no. 2 (2019): 243. The revised law provides for the transfer of use right of rural land to third parties, and it also eliminates article 43 of the previous version of the law which limited construction to state-owned (that is, urban) land—a provision that was generally viewed as the chief legal restriction preventing the emergence of a rural land market for commercial construction. See generally Qiao Shitong, "The Structure and Spirit of Chinese Property Law," in Nicole Graham, Margaret Davies, Lee Godden, eds., *Handbook of Property, Law, and Society*, New

maintains that the total area of cultivation must not fall below a "red line" of 120 million hectares.

Legally, the commodification of rural land has been accomplished by adding a new layer of rights beyond the distinction between ownership and use. The latter has been broken into a contractual right to use and a right to *control* the use. Under this new regime, as before, the collective remains the legal owner of the land. However, even after a household transfers its allocated use right, it still retains its original contractual right to that use, passing to the new owner only the right to control the use, all of which serves to uphold the ideologically indispensable claim that even landless peasants continue to enjoy an entitlement to land.

Unlike rural land conversion, which is a coercive process initiated by the state, the consolidation of agricultural land occurs through technically voluntary market transactions, nor does it result in a formal expropriation insofar as displaced peasants continue to own a contractual right to their allotment. However, although a landless household may be entitled periodically to a small check, most do not expect ever to get their land back, and in any event they have to relocate. At the same time, the consolidation of agricultural land is often managed by the state. With officials intervening to "facilitate" the process, applying varying degrees of persuasion and pressure, the rate of enclosure has been remarkable. In 2007, only 5.2 percent of China's farmland was operated by agribusiness, whereas by 2016 it had reached 35 percent.[22]

The frequent lack of proper documentation in land use transfers suggests the questionable nature of the processes by which household

---

York: Routledge, 2023. While article 63 the revised Land Administration Law does permit the transfer of rural construction land to commercial actors, it should be noted that article 82 still requires further authorization for the conversion of agricultural land to nonagricultural use.

22 Luo Qiangqiang and Joel Andreas, "Mobilizing Compliance: How the State Compels Village Households to Transfer Land to Large Farm Operators in China," *Journal of Peasant Studies* 47, no. 6 (2020): 1189.

plots have been absorbed by larger entities. In one county in Ningxia, 43 percent of the households that had transferred their land had not even signed a contract.[23] To return to the North American comparison, the consequences of the commodification of rural land in China have been broadly similar to what happened after the Dawes Act of 1887 in the United States. That act divided tribally held Indian land into individually owned allotments, making it possible to sell it to non-Indians. As a result, Indians had lost two-thirds of their land by 1934. It bears noting, again, that the use of pressure and legal trickery was an important element in the enclosure of the English commons too, and many of the strategies for dispossessing the Native Americans had already been worked out in the expropriation of English peasants.[24]

With the consolidation of farmland for industrial cultivation, capitalism has finally arrived in the countryside. Along with agribusiness, most of the land is used by large family-owned farms and specialized agricultural cooperatives, which are in turn typically dominated by commercial entities and large landowners. A peasant from Heilongjiang describes this as a return to the prerevolutionary era: "Land flows to those who are capable and they need to employ others to work for them."[25] Indeed, for the first time since the Land Reform there are again rural landlords. Peasants without the means, entrepreneurship, or social connections to become part of the new landlord class are being stratified into those that nonetheless manage to hold on to their household allotments and the rest who become agricultural laborers working on other people's land, or else have no choice but to relocate permanently. If the latter stay, they become part of a rural rather than

23 Ibid., 1197.

24 On questionable legal formalities in England, see, for example, E. C. K. Gonner, *Common Land and Inclosure* (London: Macmillan & Co., Ltd., 1912), 182.

25 Yan Hairong and Chen Yiyuan, "Agrarian Capitalization Without Capitalism? Capitalist Dynamics from Above and Below in China," *Journal of Agrarian Change* 15, no. 3 (2015): 380.

urban proletariat, but one no less dependent on markets for satisfying its material needs. Although there remains a functional differentiation between city and country, labor and land become commodities without reference to geography, marking a full transition to agrarian capitalism in China's countryside.

Enclosures Old and New

Returning to the English comparison, many dispossessed peasants in China find themselves pushed into cities much like their English counterparts were. In the case of rural land conversions, they are transformed into urbanites without even having moved, as it is the city that comes to them, colonizing the countryside. This mirrors the development of English conurbations, epitomized by London where there is a "green" or a "common" in every neighborhood, marking what was once a hamlet in its own right. And as we have seen, the Chinese peasants have responded with agitation, much as the English did, protesting against "big farmers eating small farmers"—a term perhaps even more graphic than Thomas More's characterization of the early English Enclosure Movement as "sheep eating men."[26] As E. P. Thompson observes, well into the nineteenth century "the groundswell of rural grievance came back always to access to the *land*," and so in China, too.[27]

Even the demonization of the poor has taken similar forms under English and Chinese capitalisms. Prior to the consolidation of economic class discourse, in early industrial England the unsettled "street-folk" were described in ethnic terms as "a sordid race," and London was said to be teeming with "city Arabs" and other nomads akin to "the wandering tribes" of Africa.[28] The contemporary Chinese

26 Ibid., 379 (quoting Tong Zhihui and Wen Tiejun); Thomas More, *Utopia* (London: Penguin Books, 2003).

27 E. P. Thompson, *The Making of the English Working Class* (New York: Vintage Books, 1966), 253 (emphasis in original).

28 On "commoners" as "a sordid race," see J. M. Neeson, *Commoners:*

discourse of *suzhi* likewise reserves a special disdain for the floating population in the nation's megalopolises, dismissing peasants who refuse to relocate as "lazy." While this discourse does not employ overtly racial terms, it too constitutes those with "low *suzhi*" as a different *kind* of human, rather than merely a differently situated or less fortunate compatriot.

Notwithstanding the similarities in the unfolding of English and Chinese processes of enclosure, it is equally important to attend to their historical differences. In England, the enclosure of the commons was necessary in order compel its former occupants to take on wage labor—first in commercial farming, then in rural manufacture, and finally in urban industry. The trajectory of commodification of labor in China has been distinctive. When rural industry first emerged in the 1980s, it did not entail any expropriation because it was organized in the form of collectives owned by the villagers themselves. A TVE was essentially an agricultural commons transformed into an industrial one, rather than its enclosure.

China also did not need to expropriate peasants' land in order to get them to work in *urban* industries, as evidenced by the hundreds of millions of migrant laborers who built China's modern megacities. So, for one final time: Why dispossess people who have already submitted to some of the most dehumanizing forms of industrial capitalism? This chapter has already suggested a partial answer: land finance. The expropriation of peasants can make money for local governments that are short on cash—and often also for cadres who facilitate the process and resell the right to use the land to commercial developers. But that is only a partial answer. From a larger perspective, the principal problem with

---

Common Right, Enclosure, and Social Change in England, 1700–1820 (Cambridge: Cambridge University Press, 1996), 32; on "street-folk" as "wandering tribes," see Gertrude Himmelfarb, *The Idea of Poverty: England in the Early Industrial Age* (New York: Knopf, 1985), 324; and on "city Arabs," see Saree Makdisi, *Making England Western: Occidentalism, Race, and Imperial Culture* (Chicago: University of Chicago Press, 2013).

migrant labor is that it is *incompletely proletarianized*. It depends on capital for wages, but it does not depend on wages *exclusively* for all its material needs.

So long as migrant workers are able to rely on subsistence agriculture as well, they remain at least partly independent of markets. This means that peasants make first-rate workers and second-rate consumers. Not only are some of their material needs satisfied outside of markets, but because of their precarious status and limited access to social security, they save every penny they can, as we have noted, consuming even less than they otherwise would. China's overall savings rate is said to be the highest in recorded history, and according to official statistics the Chinese citizenry consumes less than 40 percent of what it produces, a figure lower than in any other major economy in the world.[29] In the analytic vocabulary of capitalism, such a failure to consume amounts to nothing less than a crisis of "underconsumption."

So far, China has solved this problem through exports: relying on foreign consumers to buy what its factories produce. Today, export-oriented industrialization is nearing its limits as a development strategy, a process that is being accelerated further by the current US administration's war against China's trade surplus. *The ongoing enclosure of China's countryside in effect completes the proletarianization of the peasantry*. The commodification of labor has already turned it into a reserve army of labor. The commodification of rural land turns it into a reserve army of consumers as well. Dispossessed peasants become fully dependent on capital for survival, with no choice but to buy everything they need. As a peasant finding himself in the city asked, "What will we live on? Everything requires money in town."[30]

---

29 Matthew C. Klein and Michael Pettis, *Trade Wars Are Class Wars: How Rising Inequality Distorts the Global Economy and Threatens International Peace* (New Haven, CT: Yale University Press, 2020), 111.

30 Chuang and Yasuda, "Polanyi and the Peasant Question in China: State, Peasant, and Land Relations in China, 1949–Present," 331.

Finally, the greatest and most obvious difference: In England, the closing of the village commons signified a transition from feudalism to capitalism. In China, the commodification of rural land represents a transition from *socialism* to capitalism. This helps explain the belated enclosure of China's countryside. In England it was agrarian capitalism that laid the foundation for its industrial counterpart—indeed, the technologies of industrial capitalism did not even exist when English agriculture was first commercialized. In the People's Republic of China, agrarian capitalism is arriving *after* industrial capitalism. This has been possible because both were preceded by socialism. While Marx envisioned that socialism would inherit an industrialized economy from capitalism as its parting gift, Chinese state capitalism received its initial industrial foundation as a bequest from socialism. Because the PRC relied on primitive socialist accumulation, it did not need agrarian capitalism as a springboard for its industrialization. To this day, China's explosive urban growth continues to be subsidized by the legacy of rural socialism.

Yet today, China is awash with global capital, and it has plentiful labor as well. What it needs above all is *markets*. As the countryside and its population have increasingly outlived their usefulness as sites of primitive accumulation, capitalism is finally coming for the countryside. Once the proletarianization of the peasantry is complete, China too will be a nation of consumers. But what does that mean for China and the world?

Conclusion

Limits of Development in the Age of Chinese Capital

> Après moi le déluge! *is the watchword of every capitalist and of every capitalist nation.*
>
> —Karl Marx, *Capital*, vol. 1

Since 1978, China has undergone a series of seismic changes in its economic order that have radically altered its citizens' relationship to both labor and land. They have unmade the socialist working class and are in the process of expropriating the peasantry, transforming both into a propertyless proletariat. At the same time, China's political structure has not undergone a similar revolution. Accordingly, the contradiction between its systems of economic and political organization is increasingly acute. I conclude this book by summarizing key aspects China's transformation and then considering its significance, first for China's internal development and then for our global future.

The disjunctive fates of rural and urban China have been part of a single story ever since the establishment of the People's Republic. It is the impoverished hinterland that subsidized the rise of the urban industry under state socialism. Unlike in England, this development did not require the expropriation of rural land and a concomitant displacement of the peasantry. There, the Enclosure Movement provided both the capital *and* the labor for industrial development. In China, in contrast, there was no shortage of labor, and the state preferred to keep the peasants precisely where they were, rather than allowing them to flow into cities and coalesce into a potentially explosive proletariat of the kind that had become common in much of the developing world. To obtain industrial capital, the state extracted simply the economic surplus produced by the peasants while keeping the peasants themselves in place. This was the essence of primitive socialist accumulation.

After China's transition to state capitalism, the countryside has continued to subsidize urban development, supporting not only state capital but also private Chinese capital and global capital. Urban industry no longer extracts just the product of rural labor but the peasants themselves, albeit on a rotational and provisional basis. This has taken the form of a "floating population" made up of hundreds of millions of semi-proletarianized migrant workers who continue to rely in part on collectively owned, nontransferable rural land cultivated by villagers left behind. With the enclosure of rural land, China is in the process of converting its migrant labor force into permanent city-dwellers, transforming an existing reserve army of workers into a reserve army of consumers as well—making them *fully* proletarianized. Moreover, it is not only the former migrant workers who are proletarianized as their displacement becomes permanent: The arrival of agrarian capitalism proletarianizes even those who remain in the countryside.

We have already noted that the exploitation of the countryside for industrial development is emphatically not unique to China. Indeed, when viewed from a longer historical perspective, the birth of the new Chinese working class seems rather unexceptional. We have come to take it for granted that people work for wages. However, the sociologist Charles Tilly observes that as recently as 1700, only about 10 percent of the global workforce made their living by selling their labor power—"by selling themselves," in Marx's phrase—whereas today, most of us do so.[1] This is the consequence of a truly astonishing consolidation of ownership of both land and capital across the planet. As a result, most human beings have lost control over the means by which they sustain

1 Charles Tilly, "Proletarianization: Theory and Research," Working Paper, Center for Research on Social Organization, University of Michigan (1979), 3–4.

their lives. The asymmetry is stark: on the one hand, an extraordinary concentration of capital and land, and on the other, an atomized workforce made of up individual workers. The former has been made possible by advanced legal and financial technologies, while workers' efforts at unionizing are met at every turn with a corresponding array of legal, economic, and political restrictions.

As we have seen, what is distinctive about the fate of the Chinese working class is the specific way in which state socialism and state capitalism have become conjoined in China, with the former providing the foundation for the latter, as well as the temporal and spatial dimensions of this evolution. Processes of commodification of land and labor that took place over centuries in England have been compressed into just a few decades. What is more, the People's Republic of China claims an imperial footprint more encompassing than any other twentieth-century revolutionary state. Because of both the staggering speed of its transformation and its equally staggering size, China plays an oversized role in the development of global capitalism. Accordingly, the incorporation of rural and urban land, as well as rural and urban labor, into a single regime of state capitalism has both local and global implications. Ultimately it is part of a planetwide standardization of human beings' relationship to land and labor, with both humanity and nature being restructured into singular enclosed units—private individuals and private property—alienating us from the soil as well as from each other.

Let us conclude by considering some of the further social, political, and ecological consequences of the enclosure of China's countryside, for both China and the world.

Chinese Capital at Home: Contradictions of State Capitalism

The massive post-1978 reorganization of land, labor, and capital has left China with a series of internal contradictions. Perhaps the most outstanding one is the disjunction between its economic and political orders. The philosopher Jiwei Ci describes it as a contradiction between a radically new organization of desire and a largely unchanged political and ideological structure. As the state has disavowed its material responsibilities to workers, economic relations have been reconfigured as those of freedom—essentially the freedom of being left alone to fend for oneself. Ci call this "de facto freedom," a kind of freedom by default.[2] While it is negative in origin, signifying the retreat of the state rather than a result of a social struggle, it has opened the way for seeking the satisfaction of private desires. To the extent that the state wants China to become a nation of consumers, cultivating this desiring subject has become an economic imperative: While needs are limited, desires are boundless, and only desire can fuel consumption without limits.

Ci contrasts this de facto economic freedom with freedom as a positive moral or political value. In the absence of a liberal ideology valorizing it, freedom by default is not capable of giving *meaning* to material prosperity, even if one is fortunate (or well-connected) enough to have prospered in the new regime of economic inequality. It is notable, however, that the dominant language of public critique today is overwhelmingly concerned with "social justice"—associated with labor and land protests as well anti-corruption agitation more generally—rather than "democracy" or political freedom more generally. This reflects at least in part the fact that the discourse of social justice allows people to appeal to the state in terms of its own professed commitment to socialism. In some ways, this makes it, potentially, an even more damaging critique than a direct challenge to the political order. The gaping, and growing, economic inequality is a threat not only to social stability but to the very legitimacy of the regime.

At the same time, the turn to the idiom of social justice rather than Maoism is a sign of the diminished nature of Chinese socialism. As a result of four decades of "reform," there exists today, for the first time in China's history, a vast industrial proletariat of both urban and rural origin. But despite its unquestionable existence in a socioeconomic sense, it has not yet emerged as a *political* subject with a collective identity of

2 Jiwei Ci, *Moral China in the Age of Reform* (Cambridge: Cambridge University Press, 2014), 176.

the kind described by E. P. Thompson. In addition to material obstacles to labor organization, workers do not have access to an adequate public language in which to articulate their grievances.[3] As the term "class" (*jieji*) has been retired from the official lexicon, it has been replaced with euphemistic concepts such as "strata" (*jieceng*) and "vulnerable groups" (*ruoshi qunti*)—not dissimilar from the language of social movements in the United States, for example.

Consider again the transvaluation of the meaning of poverty, from a badge of honor to one of shame. This is an essentially ideological development, but no less consequential for it. The glorification of penury may be a ruse, but it can at least provide a modicum of dignity to the poor, and the subjective experience of being esteemed is surely preferable to being socially shunned. In popular discourse, this shift is reflected by the substitution of moral quality (*suzhi*) as the main criterion for social standing. No longer revered as "masters of the factory," urban workers today are stigmatized in the popular imagination for their "low *suzhi*," increasingly indistinct from rural migrants. Poverty has become not just a matter of material deprivation but a personal humiliation as well, and China's urbanization makes that humiliation hypervisible. Its cities were once defined by heavy industry—their principal raison d'être—and the bureaucracies that supervised them. Today they are shining monuments to globalization, with urban dwellers deriving their identities from what they consume rather than what they produce. What one wears and how one looks constitutes public evidence of taste and of one's *suzhi*.

Responding to these political and economic contradictions, Xi Jinping's ascendancy has coincided with the rise of neo-Maoist rhetoric.

3 One of the most notable forms worker protest has taken is *dagong shige*, a form of subaltern writing by migrant workers, often translated as "battler poetry." However, its political efficacy remains circumscribed. It is subject to state-sanction when too critical and to state-cooptation when less so. See, for example, Qin Xiaoyu, ed., *Iron Moon: An Anthology of Chinese Worker Poetry*, Eleanor Goodman trans. (Buffalo, NY: White Wine Press, 2017).

After Deng Xiaoping's singular emphasis on economic development and the need to allow some people "to get rich first," Xi Jinping is mindful of the need to balance growth with escalating demands for social justice and environmental protection, stressing the need for "common prosperity" (*gongtong fuyu*) and the construction of "an ecological civilization" (*shengtai wenming*). The invocations of ecological civilization began under Hu Jintao but are now associated with Xi, who wrote the term into China's Constitution in 2018, in symbolic recognition of the damage wrought by rural industry in particular: land and water contamination, soil erosion, environmental disease, declining food safety, the depletion of fisheries, and so on.

In the same vein, Xi has made the eradication of rural poverty one of his signature initiatives. In 2021, he declared that China had achieved a "total elimination of absolute poverty," with every village in China above the official poverty line. Yet even this victory—partly semantic, given the arbitrariness of any official definition of poverty—relied on neoliberal means, such as teaching electronic marketing to peasants and making entire villages switch to cash crops in order to raise their incomes by the announced deadline.[4] As the legal scholar Ryan Martínez Mitchell observes, what might have been a radical redistributive project turned instead into a campaign "to embed entrepreneurialism as a character trait into society at large," including rural China.[5]

Yet the state's reliance on neoliberal solutions is far from unqualified. Chinese neoliberalism is similar to the North Atlantic variant to the extent that it makes individuals responsible for themselves in economic circumstances which are beyond their control. However, it does not represent a full subsumption of the state by the logic of capital. It is a selective, strategic, and ultimately political deployment of market institutions in the service of the Party-state. China's future is therefore

4 Ryan Martínez Mitchell, "The Human Community of Fate: A Conceptual History of China's Ordoglobal Idea," *Humanity* 13, no. 2 (2022): 175–95, 186.

5 Ibid., quoting Werner Bonefeld, "Freedom and the Strong State: On German Ordoliberalism," *New Political Economy* 17, no. 5 (2012): 635.

not determined by the dictates of capital alone nor is the outcome of rural enclosure preordained. If it so desires, Chinese leadership *can* recalibrate its strategies of industrial development and rethink its current trajectory. In fact, because of its centralized structures of political authority, it is able to act more decisively than a liberal capitalist regime. Nonetheless, and despite the push and pull of policy, the long-term trend has been to continue enclosing rural land and commercializing the Chinese lifeworld.

To be sure, it is important to recognize that this trend has improved peasants' lives in significant ways. Most villages now have running water, electricity, paved roads, and internet, for example. The arrival of capital has helped diversify the rural economy. While there is great regional variation, there are villages that bear a resemblance to middle-class suburbs. On the other hand, as we have seen, even households that manage to hold on to their land in defiance of "dragonhead enterprises" and other new commercial actors become fully reliant on buying inputs from the market and cultivating crops for the market. The less fortunate landless peasants who are unable to find rural employment are in turn compelled to join the urban proletariat, even if material conditions improve for at least a subset of those who make it in the commercialized countryside.

Heeding calls by Wen Tiejun and others to find a "Third Way," some villages have sought to return to collective farming. It is indeed the case that, at least in principle, the commodification of rural land need not result in a complete predominance of private actors. If a village chooses collectively not to sell the rights to the use of its land, it can replace cultivation by individual households with a scaled-up agricultural cooperative—one in which each household exchanges its land allotment for shares in a village-based enterprise. The resulting shareholding cooperative is in some ways an agricultural version of the industrial TVE, engaging in commercial farming rather than manufacturing. As a form of self-development by the village, establishing such cooperatives is undoubtedly preferable to allowing outside commercial actors take over, yet by no means do they herald a return to the socialist collectives of the Maoist era. Even collectively owned farming enterprises are essentially commercial actors, subsumed by agrarian capitalism and relying on markets both for buying their inputs—including labor—and for selling their output.[6]

In recognition of increasing economic stratification throughout society, the state has sought to build at least a minimal safety net. In this respect, the evolution of Chinese welfare institutions has been broadly similar to the development of poor laws in England, initially enacted in response to the enclosure of the commons and the rising numbers of paupers without any means of subsistence. As the Enclosure Movement entailed the expropriation of Church property as well, poverty was transformed from an ecclesiastic concern to a secular one, becoming a social problem commanding political attention at the very top rather than a primarily theological or a local one.

At the same time, although the Elizabethan Poor Laws were motivated by an anxiety about the state of the realm as a whole, they continued to maintain a medieval commitment to territorially based charity, funded by local ratepayers and available only to paupers settled within a parish. Under the so-called settlement laws, it became as difficult for a pauper to change his official place of settlement as for a Chinese peasant under Maoism to change his *hukou* registration. By obstructing mobility, both institutions thwarted the development of a national labor market even as land was increasingly transformed into private property. In the wake of revolutionary upheaval in France, the poor laws were further fortified in 1795 by indexing welfare to the price of bread—a reform that Prime Minister George

6 Moreover, just as many of the TVEs in the 1980s were "fake"—that is, fronts for private entrepreneurs—some studies suggest that up to 85 percent of rural cooperatives are similarly "fake," or essentially private entities created for the sole purpose of collecting government subsidies intended for agricultural cooperatives. Sally Sargeson, "The Demise of China's Peasantry as a Class," *Asia Pacific Journal* 14, no. 13 (2016).

Canning credited with having "saved England from a revolution" of its own.[7]

In 1834, the New Poor Law finally abolished the centuries-old parish-based regime and replaced it with a centralized system that limited welfare strictly to the disabled and the ill. The able-bodied poor were left with no other option than the workhouse, so stigmatized and so horrific that only the truly desperate would enter it. Finally, a nationwide labor market emerged, leading to the proliferation of slums in England's industrial cities. In general outline, Xi's urbanization policies and his restricted program of social welfare envision a similar transition—except for the state's determination to prevent the emergence of slums. Even while calling for more a robust welfare system, Xi has consistently held back on public funding, preferring social security programs financed through employers and individual contributions, to prevent a fall into what he calls "the idleness-breeding trap of welfarism."[8] Welfare as such is for orphans, the disabled, and the very old, whereas the able-bodied indigent must find work, or else rely on family for support.

In England, however, the abolition of the old poor laws coincided with major political agitation. It was preceded by the Reform Act of 1832, which expanded the franchise to the middle class and opened the way to the eventual inclusion of the working class. China, in contrast, has offered no democratic reforms, nor have they been at the top of protestors' demands. On the contrary, even as the state is making its citizens turn to the market for their economic needs, it continues to appeal to the political subject of Maoism, one that is expected to sacrifice for the collective good. At the same time and somewhat improbably, the state has begun to cultivate neo-Confucian rhetoric as well. In lieu of waging class struggle, the people are called on to build a "harmonious society" (*hexie shehui*)—the less protest, the better.

---

7 Karl Polanyi, *The Great Transformation: The Political and Economic Origins of Our Time* (Boston, MA: Beacon Press, 1957), 92

8 Ya-Wen Lei, *The Gilded Cage: Technology, Development, and State Capitalism in China* (Princeton, NJ: Princeton University Press, 2023), 296.

In this vein, Xi has promoted the "Chinese dream" (*Zhongguo meng*) as the most urgent political desideratum of the millennium. This dream is not merely a Chinese rendering of its American counterpart. The American dream belongs to the individual, hearkening to the myth of Horatio Alger, whereas the Chinese dream is that of the nation. Sublating socialism into nationalism and fed by an intensive cultivation of memories of the so-called century of humiliation that followed China's defeat in the Opium Wars, it seeks to "rejuvenate" the nation and return it to its rightful place at the heart of a Sinocentric world. The realization of China's long overdue dream—one that was once a reality and now must be restored—may entail personal sacrifice, including temporary economic inequality, but everyone must play his part. This is a deferral of equality now for the sake of a future dream.

The intensifying personality cult around Xi may be interpreted as an attempt to forge unity in the absence of a political consensus, much as Mao Zedong relied on charismatic leadership to overcome social and political fragmentation. The public promotion of "Xi Jinping Thought"—it has been enshrined in the Preamble to the Constitution, along with Marxism-Leninism, Mao Zedong Thought, and Deng Xiaoping Theory—has a similar aim, although its ideological vitality remains questionable. The anthropologist John Osburg characterizes China as "a post-belief" society.[9] The People's Republic of China officially remains, and must remain, a socialist state, but its credibility in claiming that label is eroding by the day.

At the same time, the Party is losing its ability to draw on its historical legitimacy. Mao Zedong and his comrades rightfully claimed credit for having unified the nation and secured its international autonomy. In contrast, the current generation of communist princelings in charge fought no revolutionary battles but rely on inherited credentials instead. This is indeed why they appeal to a "rejuvenated" future rather than a

---

9 John Osburg, "Consuming Belief: Luxury, Authenticity, and Chinese Patronage of Tibetan Buddhism in Contemporary China," *HAU: Journal of Ethnographic Theory* 10, no. 1 (2020): 73.

revolutionary past. Ultimately the new social contract between the people and the Party-state is a pragmatic one: social stability in turn for continued economic growth, a bargain that political scientists characterize as "performance legitimacy." Herein lies the political significance of the enclosure of China's countryside. As markets for Chinese exports reach their limits and start to dwindle in the winds of what is beginning to look like a new Cold War, the belated commodification of rural land and the ongoing proletarianization of the peasantry hold the promise of delivering politically indispensable growth by creating a domestic consumer base.

With the transformation of the countryside into market society, the PRC is finally getting ready to leave behind its historical reliance on primitive modes of accumulation—both socialist and capitalist—and transition into mature capitalism.

Chinese Capital Abroad: Limits of Global Capitalism

The idea is a powerful one. As China evolves from the workshop of the world to the consumer of world, it will no longer need to rely on exploiting the countryside to fuel urban growth, bringing the post-1949 tale of two Chinas to an end. While it was once imperative to let some people "get rich first," the day is finally approaching when *everyone* can get rich—or, at a minimum, even the proletarianized working class can begin their (slow) ascent into the ranks of the middle class. One of the main cleavages in Chinese society will be overcome *and* the nation will have reestablished its economic autonomy, at least within limits allowed by the WTO.

The premise behind this dream of endless growth is an idealized theory of capitalism as an autopoietic system.[10] The final incorporation of the noncapitalist elements of the countryside will create a fully

10 For an elaboration of this idea, see Karatani Kojin, *The Structure of World History: From Modes of Production to Modes of Exchange*, Michael K. Bourdaghs trans. (Durham, NC: Duke University Press, 2014), 188.

proletarianized workforce. This workforce will not only provide labor but also buy back the commodities it produces in order to live. Although capitalism cannot set itself in motion—for that, it relies on primitive accumulation—once established, it becomes a kind of perpetual motion machine that keeps on going and growing. As the introduction observed, Rosa Luxemburg challenged Marx's notion of primitive accumulation as essentially a *pre*condition for the emergence of capitalist relations. She insisted that even the most fully developed capitalism cannot fashion surplus value out of nothing; the economy is not a system of alchemy. To continually reproduce itself, capitalism always needs an unequal outside from which to extract value. Hence primitive accumulation is not just a one-time coercive transfer of resources that provides capitalism with a start-up fund, as it were, but a permanent condition of its functioning.[11]

Luxemburg observed that one of the main obstacles to capitalism's continual expansion has been the fact that vast stretches of the earth's surface are occupied by social groups that have no desire to enter into economic relations with capitalism. This is precisely why "trading companies" such as the East India Company waged war as well as conducted trade. Luxemburg's specific concern was the crisis of underconsumption in the nineteenth century, with capital looking for new markets, and she offered her theory as an economic explanation of imperialism. It is notable that just as Lord Canning credited the late eighteenth-century system of poor relief for sparing England from a revolution in the beginning of the nineteenth century, Cecil Rhodes suggested that colonialism saved it from a civil war at the end of the century.[12]

Significantly, one of Luxemburg's main examples was China. Historically, England's problem with China was its lack of interest in

11 Rosa Luxemburg, *The Accumulation of Capital* (New Haven, CT: Yale University Press, 1951).

12 V. I. Lenin, *Imperialism: The Highest Stage of Capitalism* (Moscow: Co-operative Publishing Society of Foreign Workers in the USSR, 1934), 76, quoting Rhodes: "The Empire, as I have always said, is a bread and butter question. If you want to avoid civil war, you must become imperialists."

Western goods. As noted in chapter 4, the British ultimately solved that problem by exporting opium from India—a chemical medium that quickly produced a desire for economic exchange that had been otherwise lacking. But since this trade was illegal, China had to be coerced into it by means of the Opium Wars. Yet over time China became much more than just a market for foreign goods. It turned into a site for the expansion of capital and a source of labor as well. With respect to the most capital-intensive industry of the late nineteenth century, Western capital funded China's railroads and Chinese labor built those in the United States—in both cases, the capital was North Atlantic and the labor Chinese.

Fast forward, then, to 2001, marking China's entry into the WTO. In 1839, China was forced at gunpoint to enter into so-called free trade under the aegis of Western international law. At the turn of the millennium, it was China that waged a battle to *gain admission* into the WTO, the latest global trading regime. There is no better illustration of how profoundly China has been transformed. If the age of imperialism was the first era of globalization, the rise of the WTO symbolizes the second one. What is more, the twenty-first century variant of free trade is no less imperial that its nineteenth-century predecessor. It, too, seeks to incorporate new consumers into global trade, find new outlets for capital, and provide access to cheap labor. David Harvey calls it "the New Imperialism," for short. While distinctive from the predominantly territorial colonialisms investigated by Luxemburg, it also depends critically on primitive accumulation on a global scale, or "accumulation by dispossession," in Harvey's vocabulary.[13]

But why has China chosen to buy into its own economic subordination in the latest round of imperialism? Insofar as China wants access to global capital, it has little choice. Especially after the end of the Cold War, there are few alternatives. The Party-state has abandoned its ambitions for a global proletarian revolution, and Maoism survives today

13 David Harvey, *The New Imperialism* (Oxford: Oxford University Press, 2003).

primarily in pockets outside of China. In its stead, China has proclaimed the so-called right to development a human right—essentially a global version of letting some people(s) "get rich first." More importantly, China need not remain economically subordinated forever. What is to prevent it from becoming a New Imperialist in its own right? In just a few decades, it has gone from a chronic shortage of capital to a surplus. Indeed, that is one of the key reasons why commercial agriculture is looking so fervently to enclose the countryside. As industrial production reaches capacity, surplus capital is being invested increasingly also in speculative assets such as stocks and real estate, with financial capitalism complementing industrial capitalism and agricultural capitalism.

While the New Enclosure Movement is proceeding, it is striking that Chinese capital—both state and private—is looking for outlets beyond China's borders, such as resource extraction projects in Africa. Such projects export not only capital but often also labor, both in the form of advisers and engineers along with construction workers, miners, and relatively low-skilled labor. With the recent Belt and Road Initiative (BRI)—the largest infrastructure project ever conceived—these investments are being spread even more widely. It bears noting that this is standard operating procedure for "mature" capitalism. In England primitive accumulation began at home with the enclosure of the commons, but eventually the bulk of it was exported overseas in the form of colonialism. Running out of lands to enclose and people to dispossess at home, Chinese capital, too, is going global, setting up Sinocentric production chains in regions ranging from the Indian Ocean to Latin America.

Unsurprisingly, the Chinese government presents its debt-financed projects as the very opposite of imperialism, even as China has become world's largest creditor, surpassing the World Bank and the International Monetary Fund (IMF). Admittedly, Chinese loans typically do not target the internal structures of recipient states, unlike, say, World Bank funds that often come with a laundry list of conditions for "structural adjustment." This makes them much less objectionable politically than their Western counterparts, but not necessarily any less exploitative economically. While most loans are routed through state-controlled entities, they carry higher average interest rates than IMF and World Bank loans, although the precise terms are difficult to know as many Chinese loans contain confidentiality clauses. Often, and atypically, such loans also contain broad acceleration clauses and are collateralized by assets beyond the object of funding itself. Because the BRI is a wide umbrella encompassing numerous types of economic relationships, it is difficult to generalize about it. Many projects are no doubt desirable—at least in the view of the parties themselves—but at least some of the investments under it are akin to the forms of Treaty Port imperialism practiced by the West in China after the Opium Wars. The Hambantota International Port in Sri Lanka is perhaps the best-known example: a project funded with Chinese capital and then leased back to China for a period of ninety-nine years when Sri Lanka was unable to service its debt.[14]

The ethics of New Imperialism may be suspect, but the West is hardly in a position to question China if it wants to become a New Imperialist in its own right. Nonetheless, because of its size and global significance, China's actions have structural—indeed planetary—implications. In the first place, if China wants to export its practices of primitive accumulation elsewhere, can it find a China of its own, as it were? If it continues to expand and needs more markets and resources beyond its borders, where will they come from? Just how much "China" will a country the size of China need? Because of its sheer scale, China, like India, is not just an ordinary latecomer to the party. Its arrival will have systemic effects on global capitalism. To the extent that limitless accumulation is capitalism's transcendental logic, it can be understood as a multigenerational Ponzi scheme: a gospel of perpetual growth that generates surplus value that is transformed into capital that generates surplus value that is transformed into capital, and so on. Sadly, we

14 In fact, at least some of the reporting on it seems to have been inaccurate, but the project is certainly not the only instance of its kind. See Deborah Brautigam and Meg Rithmire, "The Chinese 'Debt Trap' Is a Myth," *The Atlantic*, February 6, 2021.

cannot all get rich—not eventually, and certainly not all at the same time. For primitive accumulation to continue to support this system, it needs people and places to dispossess, yet the commodification of land and labor have limits imposed by nature.

While some consider China's turn to reform—as the euphemism goes—as evidence of the limits of socialism, it seems more accurate to regard China's economic experience as an illustration of the ultimate limits of *development*, whether it is pursued as the supreme socialist or capitalist value, ranking above both equality and freedom. Nor should we submit to the fallacy of conflating socialism as such with state socialism, its predominant twentieth-century variant. Beyond the inherent contradictions of "socialism in one country," the planetary crisis we face today demands a truly global response, something that no state can provide alone, regardless of its internal political organization.

Insofar as we are facing the limits of development, some are looking for extraterrestrial solutions. To return to Rhodes, he proclaimed proudly, "I would annex the planets if I could"—but even he recognized that he could not.[15] Today's billionaires are less modest, with Elon Musk and Jeff Bezos reaching for the stars, seemingly ready to leave this one behind like a deflated balloon. For now, fossil fuels make it possible for us to put the equivalent of an ancient forest into a gas tank and burn it up on our drive to the grocery store—think of it as a kind of "chemical enclosure" of biomatter dating from eras long before humanity's dawn—but there is little question that our reserves are running low.

It is equally striking that billionaires aren't the only ones dreaming of an extraterrestrial solution to our predicament. Others promote a socialist version of the same in the guise of "Fully Automated Luxury Communism," advocating that we turn space, not into another commodified enclosure, but a vast new commons that will become the

15 Hannah Arendt, *The Origins of Totalitarianism* (San Diego, CA: Harcourt, 1973), 124, quoting Rhodes.

foundation for a new "post-scarcity economy."[16] To be sure, it is true—and scandalous—that the Outer Space Treaty of 1967 designates space as "the province of all mankind," yet the fact remains that, in the plainspeak of the environmentalist slogan, "There Is No Planet B." One day, the music will stop, and some generation, somewhere on this planet, will be left holding the bag.

None of this is to suggest that capitalism invented the exploitation of nature for the benefit of Homo sapiens (so called without irony). That occurred with the invention of agriculture at the latest. Even Marx's socialism is a socialist *humanism*, as the introduction observed: He defined labor as "the everlasting nature-imposed condition of human existence," whereby man "effects a change of form in the materials of nature" to satisfy his own needs.[17] To paraphrase only slightly, work is the socialist master category for describing man's struggle against nature. The ease with which Mao Zedong transformed the Great Leap Forward into a war against nature suggests as much.

Capitalism, however, takes this struggle to an altogether different level, transforming it into a *total war*. With the commodification of land, it becomes a war against *nature as such*, and with the commodification of labor a war against *humans*, too—at least the laboring ones. At the same time, the imperative of endless accumulation makes it a war without an end. There is no logical terminus when we will say, "Enough!" and declare a victory. The goal is not victory; the goal is war itself. Capitalism's capacity for, and indifference to, destruction thus far exceeds those of prior modes of production. But one thing is certain: Our war against nature *will* end. We even know how it will end: Nature will win, because it always does.

Thus we must reestablish a balanced relationship to nature and also to one another, because a natural equilibrium is not possible without some reasonable equality among humans, too. That is why the story of the

---

16 Aaron Bastani, *Fully Automated Luxury Communism* (London: Verso Books, 2019).

17 Karl Marx, *Capital*, vol. 1 (New York: Vintage Books, 1977), 284.

Chinese working class is our story as well, connecting all of us in a merciless global division of labor. Neither nature nor the Chinese are the enemy, however. Unless we restore a natural equilibrium of our own volition, the planet will do so for us. The only question is whether Homo sapiens will be part of that balance.

Depending on what we choose to do, the unmaking of the Chinese working class will be the penultimate step in our own unmaking, or it can become a wake-up call for us to remake our place in the world.

Acknowledgments

It is a truism that books take a long time to write. This book, however, is an exception, at least by my standards: I wrote the bulk of the first draft in a matter of weeks over a winter break, mostly on the second-door balcony of Waikiki Market in Honolulu. Who would have thought that this local grocery not only has the best tuna poke in town but is also a perfect setting for thinking about the past and future of global capitalism! I owe thanks to the patient staff for letting me sit around and type day after day while other customers were coming and going, keeping the cash registers humming.

Although much of the actual writing of the book took place over a compressed period of time, the process itself has taken decades. The volume covers matters I have been thinking about since the mid-eighties. That long gestation period is largely why I was able to write the book relatively fast when I finally set out to do so. That also makes it impossible for me to thank, or even be aware of, the vast number of people who have contributed to the final product. Nonetheless, I would be remiss not to mention at least a few, without in any way slighting the far more numerous people who must remain unnamed.

First of all, thanks to David L. Eng, Ania Loomba, and Joan Scott for insisting that I write this book in the first place. In 2019, I published an article in the *American Journal of Comparative Law* which laid out some of the main themes of is chapter 2 of this book.[1]

1 "People, Inc.? Law, Economic Enterprise, and the Development of Inequality in China," *American Journal of Comparative Law* 67, no. 2, 2019.

David, Ania, and Joan all insisted that I expand the article and tell the story to a larger audience. I resisted for a long time, but in the face of these formidable folks all resistance is futile—and they were of course right to keep on insisting.

It is one thing to write a manuscript and another one to publish it. A huge thank-you to Neve Gordon and Catherine Rottenberg for helping turn my ideas into a marketable proposal for Verso (and also for numerous conversations and meals). After I finished the first draft, I convened a small manuscript workshop in Brooklyn in which I received invaluable feedback from a quartet of brilliant colleagues. Thank you, Petrus Liu, Frank Upham, María Josefina Saldaña-Portillo, and Neferti Tadiar. Others who have given essential feedback on the entirety or parts of the manuscript at various stages include William Alford, Sarah Biddulph, Chen Yifeng, David Eng, Matthew Erie, James Feinerman, Mary Gallagher, Jonathan Hyslop, Chitra Joshi, Ugo Mattei, Curtis Milhaupt, Chun Peng, Shitong Qiao, Samuli Seppänen, Shuang Shen, Wang Jiangyu, Yu Xinzhong, and Taisu Zhang as well as members of Writers' Bloc, my campus writing group. Other important interlocutors include Ed Cohen, Mark Driscoll, Mae Ngai, Camille Robcis, and Hiro Yoshikawa. Needless to say, none of the above individuals are responsible for anything I say, although I have qualified many of my positions in response to their comments.

At the University of Pennsylvania, I have enjoyed the support of numerous colleagues across the fields of legal history, comparative literature, Asian studies, and beyond. In addition to those already mentioned, I am especially indebted to Chris Atwood, Angus Corbett, Jacques deLisle, Fred Dickinson, Ivan Drpić, Bill Ewald, Eric Feldman, Sally Gordon, Suvir Kaul, David Kazanjian, David Kim, Sophia Lee, Serena Mayeri, Shaun Ossei-Owusu, Sophia Rosenfeld, Beth Simmons, Paul St. Amour, Karen Tani, Andrea Wang, and Guobin Yang. I am doubly fortunate that Chris and Sophia L. also happen to be my bosses—Chris as (now former) Chair of East Asian Languages and Civilizations and Sophia as Dean of the Law School. In the field of Asian studies beyond the United States, I must single out the polymathic Michael Dutton for special thanks.

The book has benefitted from comments by audiences at several venues, including the Center for the Study of Contemporary China and the Center for East Asian Studies at Penn, the Ad Hoc Faculty Colloquium at Penn Law School, the Center for East Asian Studies at Stanford, the James E. Rogers College of Law at the University of Arizona, Cornell Law School, the Faculty of Law at the University of Hong Kong, the Faculty of Law at the National University of Singapore, the Center for Transnational Legal Studies in London, the Institute for Advanced Study at Princeton, the Institute for Advanced Study in the Humanities and Social Sciences at Tsinghua University, the U.S.-Asia Law Institute at NYU, the annual meeting of the European Association for Chinese Studies in Tallinn, the annual meeting of the European China Law Studies Association in Helsinki, the Asia Now Lecture Series at the University of Pittsburgh, and the Economic Histories of the Global South Seminar at the Indian Institute of Technology Bombay. Many thanks to all my hosts: Jacques deLisle, Beth Simmons, Jennifer Rothman, Fred Dickinson, Haiyan Lee, Xiaoqian Hu, Mitch Lasser, Chantal Thomas, Fu Hualing, Weitseng Chen, Michael Dowdle, Madhavi Sunder, Simona Novaretti, Nicola di Cosmo, Wang Hui, Hairong Yan, José Alvarez, Katherine Wilhelm, Lisa Indraccolo, Johanna Niemi, Joseph Alter, Cuilan Liu, and Zaen Alkazi. In the final stages of the project, I received critical feedback also at the Verso China conference in London in fall 2025, and I owe thanks to all the participants. I also want to acknowledge excellent research assistance by Joseph Kidd, Hongyun Yu, and Bohao Zhao.

I owe a special thank you to the *New Left Review* for publishing an advance excerpt adapted from the introduction and chapter 1 of this work.[2] Susan Watkins's phenomenal editing of that excerpt is now reflected in the final manuscript as well. Finally, I thank Sebastian Budgen at Verso for taking on this project and Michal Schatz for supporting it all the way to completion.

2 "The Making of the Chinese Working Class," *New Left Review* 151: January–February 2025.

I dedicated my last book to my mother, Liisa Sjöstedt—the most avid reader ever, who has evidently passed her reading gene to me. This book is dedicated to David Eng, an interlocutor extraordinaire who has been my comrade-in-life for the past quarter of a century and counting.

Chinese Glossary

caizheng baogan 财政包干
chengbao jingying zeren zhi 承包经营责任制
chi daguo fan 吃大锅饭
chushen 出身
cungui minyue 村规民约
cunmin weiyuanhui 村民委员会
dachanquan 大产权
dagong 打工
dagongzai 打工仔
dagongmei 打工妹
dagong shige 打工诗歌
da guimo qunti shijian 大规模群体事件
da jiating 大家庭
danwei 单位
dingti 顶替
dingzihu 钉子户
fenzao chifan 分灶吃饭
getihu 个体户
gongchang de zhuren 工厂的主人
gongren 工人
gongsihua 公司化
gongtong fuyu 共同富裕
gongye fanbu nongye 工业反哺农业
gongzhang 工长
guanggun 光棍
gufen hezuo qiye 股份合作企业

hexie shehui 和谐社会
hong maozi 红帽子
hukou 户口
huomai 活卖
jiating lianchan chengbao zhi 家庭联产承包制
jieji 阶级
jieceng 阶层
juntian zhidu 均田制度
litu bulixiang 离土不离乡
liudong renkou 流动人口
liumangzui 流氓罪
liumang 流氓
neibu de disan shijie 内部的第三世界
neizhao 内招
nongmin 农民
nongmin fudan 农民负担
nongmin-gong 农民工
nongye shengyu laodongli 农业剩余劳动力
popo duo 婆婆多
quanmin suoyouzhi gongye qiye 全民所有制工业企业
rang nongmin shanglou 让农民上楼
rang ziben dao nongcun qu 让资本到农村去
ruoshi qunti 弱势群体
shehuizhuyi chuji jieduan 社会主义初级阶段
shehuizhuyi shichang jingji 社会主义市场经济
shehui zhuyi xin nongcun 社会主义新农村
shengtai wenming 生态文明
shidi nongmin 失地农民
shei touzi, shei suoyou, shei shouyi 谁投资，谁所有，谁收益
shouzu jieji 收租阶级
siyouhua 私有化
si hai 四害
suoyouzhi gaizao 所有制改造
suzhi 素质
tongzhao tongpei 统招统配
tudi caizheng 土地财政

tudi huan shebao 土地换社保
wo buzuo lirun 我不做利润
wuchanzhe 无产者
xiahai 下海
xiangzhen qiye 乡镇企业
xiaochanquan 小产权
xincheng 新城
xin quandi yundong 新圈地运动
xinxing chengzhenhua guihua 新型城镇化规划
xin tudi zhidu gaige 新土地制度改革
yichang weijia 以厂为家
yitian liangzhu 一田两主
zhengqi fenkai 政企分开
Zhongguo meng 中国梦
zhuada, fangxiao 抓大放小
zong jingli 总经理

Select Bibliography, Excluding Works Cited in the Text

Alexander, Lewis M. "The Ocean Enclosure Movement." *San Diego Law Review* 20 (1983): 561–94.

Alford, William P. and Yuanyuan Shen. "Have You Eaten, Have You Divorced? Debating the Meaning of Marriage in China." In William C. Kirby ed., *Realms of Freedom in Modern China*. Stanford, CA: Stanford University Press, 2004.

Anderson, Perry. *Lineages of the Absolutist State*. London: Verso Books, 2013.

Anderson, Perry. *Passages from Antiquity to Feudalism*. London: Verso Books, 2013.

Anderson, Perry. "Two Revolutions." *New Left Review* 61 (January/February, 1990): 59–96.

Andreas, Joel and Shaohua Zhan. "*Hukou* and Land: Market Reform and Rural Displacement in China." *Journal of Peasant Studies* 43, no. 4 (2016): 798–827.

Berman, Harold J. *Justice in the U.S.S.R.: An Interpretation of Soviet Law*, rev. ed. Cambridge, MA: Harvard University Press, 1963.

Bernstein, Henry. "Some Reflections on Agrarian Change in China." *Journal of Agrarian Change* 15, no. 3, (2015): 454–77.

Bernstein, Thomas P. and Xiaobo Lu. "Extracting Funds from the Peasants." In *Taxation Without Representation in Rural China*. Cambridge: Cambridge University Press, 2008.

Bian, Yanjie. *Work and Inequality in Urban China*. Albany, NY: SUNY Press, 1994.

Biddulph, Sarah, Sean Cooney, and Ying Zhu. *Law and Fair Work in China*. London: Routledge, 2013.

Blaustein, Albert B., ed. *Fundamental Legal Documents of Communist China*. South Hackensack, NJ: Fred B. Rothman & Co, 1962.

Bramall, Chris. *Chinese Economic Development*. Abingdon: Routledge, 2009.

Brook, Timothy and Gregory Blue. *China and Historical Capitalism: Genealogies of Sinological Knowledge*. Cambridge: Cambridge University Press, 2009.

Brown, Elizabeth, R. "The Tyranny of a Construct: Feudalism and Historians of Medieval Europe." *American Historical Review* 79, no. 4 (1974): 1063–88.

Brown, Jeremy. *City Versus Countryside in Mao's China: Negotiating the Divide*. Cambridge: Cambridge University Press, 2012.

Chan, Anita and Jonathan Unger. "A Chinese State Enterprise Under the Reforms: What Model of Capitalism?" *China Journal* 62 (July 2009): 1–26.

Chao, Kang. *Man and Land in Chinese History: An Economic Analysis*. Stanford, CA: Stanford University Press, 1968.

Che, Jiahua and Yingyi Qian. "Insecure Property Rights *and* Government Ownership of Firms." *Quarterly Journal of Economics* 113, no. 2 (1998): 467–96.

Chen, Chih-Joy Jay. *Transforming Rural China: How Local Institutions Shape Property Rights in China*. New York: Routledge, 2004.

Christiansen, Flemming and Junzuo Zhang. *Village, Inc: Chinese Rural Society in the 1990s*. Honolulu: University of Hawaii Press, 1998.

Chuang, Julia. *Beneath the China Boom: Labor, Citizenship, and the Making of a Rural Labor Market*. Oakland: University of California Press, 2020.

Coase, Ronald and Ning Wang. *How China Became Capitalist*. New York: Palgrave Macmillan, 2012.

Creemers, Rogier and Susan Trevaskes, eds., *Law and the Party in China: Ideology and Organization*. Cambridge: Cambridge University Press, 2020.

Cui, Wei. *The Administrative Foundations of the Chinese Fiscal State*. Cambridge: Cambridge University Press, 2022.

Cui, Zhiyuan. "Whither China? The Discourse on Property Rights in the Chinese Reform Context." *Social Text* (1998): 67–81.

Davis, Kathleen. *Periodization and Sovereignty: How Ideas of Feudalism and Secularization Govern the Politics of Time*. Philadelphia: University of Pennsylvania Press, 2017.

Dirlik, Arif. *Revolution and History: Origins of Marxist Historiography in China, 1919–1937*. Berkeley: University of California Press, 1989.

Du, Yue. *State and Family in China: Filial Piety and Its Modern Reform.* Cambridge: Cambridge University Press, 2022.

Dutton, Michael. *The Book of Politics: China in Theory*. Durham, NC: Duke University Press, 2024.

Eng, David, Teemu Ruskola, and Shuang Shen, eds., *China and the Human.* Special double-issue of *Social Text* 29, no. 4 (2012): 1–27.

Epstein, Edward J. and Ye Lin. "Individual Enterprise in Contemporary Urban China: A Legal Analysis of Status and Regulation." *International Lawyer* 21, no. 2 (1987): 397–436.

Estlund, Cynthia. *A New Deal for China's Workers?* Cambridge, MA: Harvard University Press, 2017.

Eyferth, Jacob. "State Socialism and the Rural Household: How Women's Handloom Weaving (and Pig-Raising, Firewood-Gathering, Food-Scavenging) Subsidized Chinese Accumulation." *International Review of Social History* 67, no. 2 (2022): 213–49.

Fang, Hanmin. "The Chinese Pension System." National Bureau of Economic Research Working Paper Series, no. 25088, Cambridge, MA, 1998.

Fang, Liufang. "China's Corporatization Experiment." *Duke Journal of Comparative and International Law* 5, no. 2 (1995): 149–269.

Farrer, James. *Opening Up: Youth Sex Culture and Market Reform in Shanghai.* Chicago: University of Chicago Press, 2002.

Farquhar, Judith. *Appetites: Food and Sex in Post-Socialist China*. Durham, NC: Duke University Press, 2002.

Faure, David. *China and Capitalism: A History of Business Enterprise in Modern China*. Hong Kong: University of Hong Kong Press, 2006.

Federici, Silvia. *Reproduction at Point Zero: Housework, Reproduction, and Feminist Struggle*. Oakland, CA: PM Press, 2020.

Fei, Hsiao-tung [Fei Xiaotong]. "Financing China's Rural Industrialization." *China Economist*, August 2, 1848: 108–13.

Fransceschine, Ivan and Christian Sorace, eds., *Proletarian China: A Century of Chinese Labour*. New York: Verso Books, 2022.

Frazier, Mark W. *Socialist Insecurity: Pensions and the Politics of Uneven Development in China*. Ithaca, NY: Cornell University Press, 2010.

Fu, Hualing and John Gillespie, eds., *Resolving Land Disputes in East Asia: Exploring the Limits of Law*. Cambridge: Cambridge University Press, 2014.

Fu, Tingmei. "Legal Person in China: Essence and Limits." *American Journal of Comparative Law* 41, no. 2 (1993): 261–97.

Gabriele, Alberto. *Enterprise, Industry, and Innovation in the People's Republic of China: Questioning Socialism from Deng to the Trade and Tech War*. Singapore: Springer, 2020.

Gallagher, Mary. *Authoritarian Legality in China: Law, Workers, and the State*. Cambridge: Cambridge University Press, 2017.

Gao, Henry and Gregory Shaffer. "A New Chinese Economic Order?" *Journal of International Economic Law* 28 (2020): 607–35.

Goldman, Wendy Z. "Introduction: Primitive Accumulation and Socialism." *International Review of Social History* 67, no. 2 (2022): 195–209.

Goodman, Bryna. *Native Place, City, and Nation: Regional Networks and Identities in Shanghai, 1853–1937*. Berkeley: University of California Press, 1995.

Green, Stephen. "Privatization in the Former Soviet Bloc: Has China Learned the Lessons?" In Stephen Green and Guy S. Liu, eds., *Exit the Dragon: Privatization and State Control in China*. Malden, MA: Blackwell Publishing, 2005.

Harrison, Henrietta. "Village Industries and the Making of Rural-Urban Difference in Early Twentieth-Century Shanxi." In Jacob Eyferth ed., *How China Works: Perspectives on the Twentieth-Century Industrial Workplace*. New York: Routledge, 2006.

Hayward, Jane. "Beyond the Ownership Question: Who Will Till the Land? The New Debate on China's Agricultural Production." *Critical Asian Studies* 49, no. 4 (2017): 523–45.

He, Xin. "Street as Courtroom: State Accommodation of Labor Protest in South China." *Law and Society Review* 44, no. 1 (2020): 157–84.

Hell, Natalie and Scott Rozelle. *Invisible China: How the Urban Rural Divide Threatens China's Rise*. Chicago: University of Chicago Press, 2020.

Hertz, Ellen. *The Trading Crowd: An Ethnography of the Shanghai Stock Market*. Cambridge: Cambridge Chicago: University Press, 2002.

Ho, Samuel P. S. and George C. S. Lin. "Emerging Land Markets in Rural and Urban China: Policies and Practices." *The China Quarterly* 175 (2003): 681–707.

Hobsbawm, Eric, ed. *Pre-Capitalist Economic Formations: Marx*. New York: International Publishers, 1965.

Hobson, John A. *Imperialism: A Study*. New York: Gordon Press, 1975.

Holcombe, Randall G. *The Concept of Political Capitalism*. Cambridge: Cambridge University Press, 2018.

Hong, Sheng and Zhao Nong. *China's State-Owned Enterprises: Nature, Performance, and Reform*. Singapore: World Scientific Publishing, 2013.

Hsu, Carolyn L. *Creating Market Socialism: How Ordinary People Are Shaping Class and Status in China*. Durham, NC: Duke University Press, 2007.

Huang, Philip C. C. *Code, Custom, and Legal Practice in China: The Qing and the Republic Compared*. Stanford, CA: Stanford University Press, 2001.

Huang, Mingwei. *Reconfiguring Racial Capitalism: South Africa in the Chinese Century*. Durham, NC: Duke University Press, 2024.

Huang, Yasheng. *Capitalism with Chinese Characteristics: Entrepreneurship and the State*. Cambridge: Cambridge University Press, 2008.

Hung, Ho-fung. *The China Boom: Why China Will Not Rule the World*. New York: Columbia University Press, 2016.

Karl, Rebecca. *Mao Zedong and China in the Twentieth-Century World*. Durham, NC: Duke University Press, 2010.

Kirby, William C. "The Nationalist Regime and the Chinese Party-State, 1928–1958." In Merle Goldman and Andrew Gordon, eds., *Historical Perspectives on Contemporary East Asia*. Cambridge, MA: Harvard University Press, 2000, 211–37.

Kong, Travis. *Sexuality and the Rise of China*. Durham, NC: Duke University Press, 2023.

Kornai, Janos. *The Socialist System: The Political Economy of Communism*. Princeton, NJ: Princeton University Press, 1992.

Kun, Bela. *Fundamental Laws of the Chinese Soviet Republic, with an Introduction*. New York: International Publishers, 1934.

Lee, Ching Kwan. *The Specter of Global China: Politics, Labor, and Foreign Investment in Africa*. Chicago: University of Chicago Press, 2017.

Lee, Ching Kwan. "The Unmaking of the Chinese Working Class in the Northeastern Rustbelt." In Ching Kwan Lee ed., *Working in China: Ethnographies of Labor and Workplace Transformation*. New York: Routledge, 2006, 15–37.

Lee, Haiyan. *Revolution of the Heart: A Genealogy of Love in China*. Stanford, CA: Stanford University Press, 2006.

Lenin, Vladimir Ilyich. *The State and Revolution*. Chicago, IL: Haymarket Books, 2014.

Levy, Katja and Knut Pißler. *Charity with Chinese Characteristics: Chinese Charitable Foundations Between the Party-State and Society*. London: Edward Elgar Publishing, 2020.

Li, David D. "A Theory of Ambiguous Property Rights in Transition Economies: The Case of the Chinese Non-State Sector." *Journal of Comparative Economics* 23, no. (1996): 1–19.

Li, Hongbin and Scott Rozelle. "Privatizing Rural China: Insider Privatization, Innovative Contracts, and the Performance of TVEs." *The China Quarterly* 176 (2004): 981–1005.

Li, Huaiyin. *Village China Under Socialism and Reform*. Stanford, CA: Stanford University Press, 2009.

Li, Ju. "From 'Master' to 'Loser': Changing Working Class Cultural Identity in Contemporary China." *International Labor and Working Class History* 88 (2015): 190–208.

Lin, Chun. *China and Global Capitalism: Reflections on Marxism, History, and*

Lin, George C. S. *Developing China: Land, Politics, and Social Conditions*. London, New York: Routledge, 2009.

Lin, Li-wen and Curtis Milhaupt. "We Are the (National) Champions: Understanding the Mechanisms of State Capitalism in China." *Stanford Law Review* 65 (2013): 697–759.

Lin, Nan. "Local Market Socialism: Local Corporatism in Action in Rural China." *Theory and Society* 24, no. 3 (1995): 301–54.

Linebaugh, Peter. *Stop, Thief! The Commons, Enclosures, and Resistance*. Oakland, CA: PM Press, 2014.

Linklater, Andro. *Owning the Earth: The Transforming History of Land Ownership*. New York: Bloomsbury USA, 2013.

Liu, Petrus. *The Specter of Materialism: Queer Theory and Marxism in the Age of Beijing Consensus*. Durham, NC: Duke University Press, 2023.

Liu, Xiaoyuan. *Frontier Passages: Ethnopolitics and the Rise of Chinese Communism, 1921–1945*. Stanford, CA: Stanford University Press, 2004.

Lötveit, Trygve. *Chinese Communism 1931–1934: Experience in Civil Government*. London: Curzon Press, 1978.

Love, John. *Antiquity and Capitalism: Max Weber and the Sociological Foundations of Roman Civilization*. New York: Routledge, 1991.

Luo, Qiangqiang, Joel Andreas and Yao Li. "Grapes of Wrath: Twisting Arms to Get Villagers to Cooperate with Agribusiness in China." *The China Journal* 77 (2016): 27–50.

Macpherson, C. B. *The Political Theory of Possessive Individualism: From Hobbes to Locke*. Oxford: Clarendon Press, 1962.

Manning, Kimberley Ens. *The Party Family: Revolutionary Attachments and the Gendered Origins of State Power in China*. Ithaca, NY: Cornell University Press, 2023.

Mandel, Ernest. *Marxist Economic Theory*, vol. 1. New York: Monthly Review Press, 1971.

Mao, Tse-tung [Mao Zedong]. *Selected Works of Mao Tse-tung*. Beijing: Foreign Languages Press, 1975.

Marquis, Christopher and Kunyan Qiao. *The Communist Roots of Chinese Enterprise*. New Haven, CT: Yale University Press, 2022.

Milhaupt, Curtis and Wentong Zheng. "Beyond Ownership: State Capitalism and the Chinese Firm." *Georgetown Law Journal* 103 (2015): 665–722.

Moore, Barrington Jr. *Social Origins of Dictatorship and Democracy: Lord and Peasant in the Making of the Modern World*. Boston, MA: Beacon Press, 1993.

Nee, Victor and Sonja Opper. *Capitalism from Below: Markets and Institutional Challenge in China*. Cambridge, MA: Harvard University Press, 2012.

Ngai, Pun. *Made in China: Women Factory Workers in a Global Workplace*. Durham, NC: Duke University Press, 2005.

Ngai, Pun. "Discursive Dyslexia and the Articulation of Class: A Theoretical Perspective on China's Young Female Migrant Workers (*Dagongmei*)." In Chongqing Wu, *Mapping China: Peasants, Migrant Workers, and Informal Labor*. Leiden: Brill Publishers, 2016, 80–102.

Ngai, Pun. "State Meets Capital: The Making and Unmaking of a New Chinese Working Class." In Pun Ngai ed., *Made in China: Women Factory Workers in a Global Market Place*. Durham, NC: Duke University Press, 2005, 23–48.

North, Douglass. *Gunnar Myrdal Lecture: The Role of Institutions in Economic Development*. United Nations Economic Commission for Europe, Occasional Paper No. 1, 2003.

Oi, Jean. *State and Peasant in Contemporary China: The Political Economy of Village Government*. Berkeley: University of California Press, 1989.

Oi, Jean, ed. *Going Private in China: The Politics of Corporate Restructuring and System Reform*. Lanham, MD: Rowman & Littlefield Publishers, 2011.

Oi, Jean. "The Chinese Village, Inc." In Bruce Reynolds ed., *Chinese Economic Policy: Economic Reform at Midstream*. New York: Paragon House, 1988.

Osburg, John. *Anxious Wealth: Money and Morality Among China's New Rich*. Stanford, CA: Stanford University Press, 2013.

Palmer, Michael. "Transforming Family Law in Post-Deng China: Marriage, Divorce, and Reproduction." *The China Quarterly* 191 (2007): 675–95.

Pei, Xiaolin. "Township-Village Enterprises, Local Governments, and Rural Communities The Chinese Village as a Firm During Economic Transition." *Economics of Transition* 4, no. 1 (1996): 43–66.

Perry, Elizabeth J. "From Mass Campaigns to Managed Campaigns: 'Constructing a New Socialist Countryside.' " In Elizabeth J. Perry and Sebastian Heilman, eds., *Mao's Invisible Hand*. Cambridge, MA: Harvard University Press, 2011, 30–61.

Potter, Sulamith Heins and Jack M. Potter. *China's Peasants: The Anthropology of a Revolution*. Cambridge: Cambridge University Press, 1990.

Preobrazhensky, Evgeny. *The New Economics*. Oxford: Clarendon Press, 1965.

Qian, Yingyi and Joseph Stiglitz. "Institutional Innovation and the Role of Local Government in Transition of Economies." In John McMillan and Barry Naughton, eds., *Reforming Asian Socialism: The Growth of Market Institutions*. Ann Arbor: University of Michigan Press, 1996.

Qian, Yingyi and Barry Weingast. "Institutions, State Activism, and Economic Development: A Comparison of State-Owned and Township-Village Enterprises in China." In Masahiki Aoki, Hyung-yi Kim, and Masahiro Okuno-Fujiwara, eds., *The Role of Government in East Asian Development: Comparative Institutional Analysis*. Oxford: Oxford University Press, 1997.

Qiao, Shitong. *Chinese Small Property: The Co-evolution of Law and Social Norms*. Cambridge: Cambridge University Press, 2025.

Rithmire, Meg E. *Land Bargains and Chinese Capitalism: The Politics of Property Rights under Reform*. Cambridge: Cambridge University Press, 2015.

Rodenbiker, Jesse. *Ecological States: Politics of Science and Nature in Urbanizing China*. Ithaca, NY: Cornell University Press, 2023.

Rofel, Lisa. *Desiring China: Experiments in Neoliberalism, Sexuality, and Public Culture*. Durham, NC: Duke University Press, 2007.

Rong, Tao. "Employees' Property Rights in China's State-Owned Enterprise Reorganization." *Columbia Journal of Asian Law* 13, no. 2 (1999): 153.

Ruskola, Teemu. "Law, Sexual Morality, and Gender Equality in Qing and Communist China." *Yale Law Journal* 103 (1994): 2531–565.

Ruskola, Teemu. "Conceptualizing Corporations and Kinship: Comparative Law and Development Theory in a Chinese Perspective." *Stanford Law Review* 52, no. 6 (2000): 1599–729.

Ruskola, Teemu. "What Is a Corporation? Liberal, Confucian, and Socialist Theories of Enterprise Organization (and State, Family, and Personhood)," *Seattle University Law Review* 37 (2014): 637–64.

Ruskola, Teemu. "The Dao of Mao: Sinocentric Socialism and the Politics of International Legal Theory." In Matthew Craven, Sundhya Pahuja, and Gerry Simpson, eds., *International Law and the Cold War*. Cambridge: Cambridge University Press, 2020.

Saito, Kohei. *Karl Marx's Ecosocialism: Capital, Nature, and the Unfinished Critique of Political Economy*. New York: Monthly Review Press, 2017.

Sargeson, Sally. "Violence as Development: Land Expropriation and China's Urbanization." *Journal of Peasant Studies* 40, no. 6 (2013): 1063–85.

Schipani, Cindy and Junhai Liu. "Corporate Governance in China: Then and Now." *Columbia Business Law Review* (2002): 1–69.

Schneider, Mindi. "What, Then, Is a Chinese Peasant? *Nongmin* Discourses and Agroindustrialization in Contemporary China." *Agriculture and Human Values* 32 (2015): 331–46.

Schram, Stuart. *The Political Thought of Mao Tse-tung*, revised edition. New York: Praeger Publishers, 1969.

Scott, James C. *The Moral Economy of the Peasant: Rebellion and Subsistence in Southeast Asia*. New Haven, CT: Yale University Press: 1977.

Shao, Qin. *Shanghai Gone: Domicide and Defiance in a Chinese Megacity*. Lanham, MD: Rowman & Littlefield Publishers, 2013.

Shapiro, Judith. *Mao's War Against Nature: Politics and the Environment in Revolutionary China*. Cambridge: Cambridge University Press, 2001.

Shi, Chenxia. *Political Determinants of Corporate Governance in China*. London: Routledge, 2013.

Shih, Shu-mei. "Race and Relation: The Global Sixties in the South of the South." *Comparative Literature* 68, no. 2 (2016): 141–54.

Shirk, Susan. *The Political Logic of Economic Reform in China*. Los Angeles: University of California Press, 1993.

Simon, William H. "The Legal Structure of the Chinese 'Socialist Market' Enterprise." *Journal of Corporation Law* 21 (1996): 267–306.

Smith, Nick R. *The End of the Village: Planning the Urbanization of Rural China*. Minneapolis: University of Minnesota Press, 2021.

Smith, Nick R. "One Village, One Product: Agro-industrial Village Corporatism in Contemporary China." *Journal of Agrarian Change* 19, no. 2 (2018): 249–69.

Solinger, Dorothy J. *Chinese Business Under Socialism: The Politics of Domestic Commerce in Contemporary China*. Berkeley: University of California Press, 1987.

Solinger, Dorothy. *Poverty and Pacification: The Chinese State Abandons the Old Working Class*. Lanham, MD: Rowman & Littlefield, 2022.

Stalin, Joseph. *Marxism and the National and Colonial Question*. Honolulu, HI: University Press of the Pacific, 2003.

Stern, Nicholas and Joseph Stiglitz. "Reform from a Comparative Perspective." In Peter J. Hammond and Gareth D. Myles, eds., *Incentives, Organization, and Public Economics*. Oxford: Oxford University Press, 2000.

Stiglitz, Joseph. *Whither Socialism?* Cambridge, MA: Massachusetts Institute of Technology Press, 1994.

Stiglitz, Joseph. "Quis Custodiet Ipsos Custodes?" *Challenge* 42, no. 6 (1999): 26–67.

Sun, Laixiang. "Evolving and Functioning Mechanisms of Employee Stock Ownership in China's Township and Village Enterprises." In Laixiang Sun ed., *Ownership and Governance of Enterprises: Recent Innovative Developments*. London: Palgrave Macmillan Press, 2003.

Sun, Xinhua. 2014. "Nongye Qiyehua yu Nongmin Ban Wuchanhua: Gongshang Qiye Liuzhuan Nongdi dui Nongcun Shengchan Guanxi de Zaizao [Agricultural Industrialization and Semi-Proletarianization of Farmers: Reconstruction of Rural Relations of Production Through Transfer of Farmland by Industrial and Commercial Enterprises]." *Zhongguo Yanjiu* [*China Research*] 2 (2003): 162–84.

Tadiar, Neferti. *Remaindered Life*. Durham, NC: Duke University Press, 2022.

Tilly, Charles. "Flows of Capital and Forms of Industry in Europe, 1500–1900." *Theory and Society* 12, no. 2 (1983): 123–42.

Tomasic, Roman, Wang Fuming, Zhao Xudong, and Ma Zong, eds., *Corporate Governance: Challenges for China*, 2005.

Tooze, Adam. *Crashed: How a Decade of Financial Crises Changed the World*. New York: Viking, 2018.

Tsai, Kellee S. *Back Alley Banking: Private Entrepreneurs in China*. Ithaca, NY: Cornell University Press, 2002.

Upham, Frank. *The Great Property Fallacy: Theory, Reality, and Growth in Developing Countries*. Cambridge: Cambridge University Press, 2018.

Volland, Nicolai. "Turning the Tables on the Global North: China, Afro-Asia, and Cold War Cultural Diplomacy." In Lisa Rofel and Carlos Rojas, eds., *New World Orderings: China and the Global South*, 2022, 21–37.

Walder, Andrew. "The Remaking of the Chinese Working Class, 1949–1981." *Modern China* 10, no. 1 (1984): 3–48.

Walder, Andrew. "Local Governments as Industrial Firms: An Organizational Analysis of China's Transitional Economy." *American Journal of Sociology* 101, no. 2 (1995): 263–302.

Wallerstein, Immanuel. *The Modern World System: Capitalist Agriculture and the Origins of the European World Economy in the Sixteenth Century*. Berkeley: University of California Press, 2011.

Walter, Carl E. and Fraser J. T. Howie. *Red Capitalism: The Fragile Financial Foundation of China's Extraordinary Rise*. Singapore: John Wiley & Sons, 2012.

Wang, Alex L. *Chinese Global Environmentalism*. Cambridge: Cambridge University Press, 2026.

Wang, Fei-Ling. *Organizing Through Division and Exclusion: China's Hukou System*. Stanford, CA: Stanford University Press, 2005.

Wang, Hui. *China's New Order: Society, Politics, and Economy in Transition*. Cambridge, MA: Harvard University Press, 2003.

Wang, Hui. *China's Twentieth-Century: Revolution, Retreat, and the Road to Equality*. New York: Verso Books, 2016.

Wang, Hui. "The Crisis of Representativeness and Post-Party Politics." *Modern China* 40, no. 2 (2014): 214–39.

Wang, Jiangyu and Cheng-Han Tan. "Mixed Ownership Reform and Corporate Governance in China's State-Owned Enterprises." *Vanderbilt Journal of Transnational Law* 53 (2020): 1055–107.

Wang, Wen and Fangzhi Ye. "The Political Economy of Land Finance in China." *Public Budgeting and Finance* 36, no. 2 (2015): 91–110.

Wang, Zhaofeng. "Corporate Governance Under State Control: The Chinese Experience." *Theoretical Inquiries in Law* 13, no. 2 (2012): 487–502.

Wank, David. *Commodifying Communism: Business, Trust, and Politics in a Chinese City*. Cambridge: Cambridge University Press, 2001.

Weaver, John C. *The Great Land Rush and the Making of the Modern World, 1650–1900*. Montreal: McGill-Queen's University Press, 2006.

Wei, John. *Queer Chinese Cultures and Mobilities: Kinship, Migration, and Middle Classes*. Hong Kong: Hong Kong University Press, 2020.

Weitzman, Martin L. and Chenggang Xu. "Chinese Township-Village Enterprises as Vaguely Defined Cooperatives." *Journal of Comparative Economics* 18 (1994): 121–45.

Wen, Tiejun and Yang Shuai. "Jingji Bodong, Caishui Tizhi Bianqian yu Tudi Ziyuan Zibenhua: Dui Zhongguo Gaige Kaifang Yilan 'Sanci Quandi' Xiangguan Wenti de Shizheng Fen [Economic Fluctuation, Fiscal Reform, and the Capitalization of Land Resources: An Empirical Analysis of 'Three Waves of Enclosure' in China since Reform and Opening Up]. *Jingli Shijie* [Management World] 4 (2010): 32–41.

Whiting, Susan H. *Power and Wealth in Rural China: The Political Economy of Social Change*. Cambridge: Cambridge University Press, 2000.

Williams, Harry. "Property Rights and Legal Reform in Township and Village Enterprises in China." *Asia-Pacific Law and Policy Journal* 2, no. 1 (2001): 249.

Williams, Raymond. *The Country and the City*. Oxford: Oxford University Press, 1973.

Wolf, Eric R. *Peasant Wars of the Twentieth Century*. New York: Harper & Row, 1969.

Woo, Margaret Y. K. "Shaping Citizenship: Chinese Family Law and Women." *Yale Journal of Law and Feminism* 15, no. 1 (2003): 99–134.

Wu, Yiching. *The Cultural Revolution at the Margins: Chinese Socialism in Crisis*. Cambridge, MA: Harvard University Press, 2014.

Wu, Mark. "The 'China, Inc.' Challenge to Global Trade Governance." *Harvard Journal of International Law* 57 (2016): 261–324.

Xi, Chao. *Corporate Governance and Legal Reform in China*. London: Wildy, Simmons & Hill Publishing, 2009.

Xiao, Qin. *The Theory of the Firm and Chinese Enterprise Reform*. London: Routledge, 2004.

Xu, Yong. "Zhuangyuan Jingji [Manor Economy]." *Xuexi yu Shijian* [Study and Practice] 9, no. 7 (2002): 15–16.

Yan, Hairong. "Spectralization of the Rural: Reinterpreting the Labor Mobility of Rural Young Women in Post-Mao China." *American Ethnologist* 30, no. 4 (2003): 578–96.

Yelling, J. A. *Common Field and Enclosure in England 1450–1850*. Hamden, CT: Archon Books, 1977.

Zarrow, Peter. *China in War and Revolution 1895–1949*. New York: Routledge, 2005.

Zhan, Shaohua. *The Land Question in China: Agrarian Capitalism, Industrious Revolution, and East Asian Development*. Abingdon: Routledge, 2019.

Zhang, Charlie Yi. *Dreadful Desires: The Uses of Love in Neoliberal China*. Durham, NC: Duke University Press, 2022.

Zhang, Forrest Q. and John A. Donaldson. "From Peasants to Farmers: Peasant Differentiation, Labor Regimes, and Land-Rights Institutions in China's Agrarian Transition." *Politics and Society* 38, no. 4 (2010): 458–89.

Zhong, Yang. *Local Government and Politics in China: Challenges from Below*. Armonk, NY: M. E. Sharpe, 2003.

Index